The Mobility Project, Adventures in Humanitarian Work

BY

DANNY QUINTANA
and LISA MURPHY

Copyright © 2021 by Danny Quintana and Lisa Murphy
All rights reserved.
ISBN:979-858329203-5

8-11-21

To Carole & Tom
Best wishes always

For ~~my Tia~~ Celsa Quintana, my wonderful aunt who set the standard for humility, patience and kindness. Thank you for helping me as a young child after my mother Amelia Blea Quintana's death. Your guidance and example should be followed by all. Rest in peace with the Lord and all who have gone before us. Your prayers worked wonders.

For my mom and dad, Lynn and Paul Gonder. Thank you for your constant support and unconditional love, always. Your willingness to love and accept our fall from Grace goes… beyond all else. In your ability to trust our love for God, you both learned to love Him yourselves. This shows me that you saw God's greatness before your very eyes. I am most grateful for this. Rest in Peace Dad. I love and appreciate you and Mom more than you will ever know.

savingoceans.org
danyquintanawriter@gmail

Acknowledgements

It is impossible to have delivered so many wheelchairs all over the world without the incredible help of the Lord. Thanks to Hope Haven for providing us thousands of wheelchairs to give out to the world's poor and disabled. Thanks to our families for your patience while we were out in the field. And thanks to all of the following: Joni Eareckson Tada Foundation; Mark Richard, Isaac and Natalie Quintana and the Quintana Family Trust; Shawna, Ryan, Aaron Murphy, Richard St Denis, Alex Rice; Brock Moller, Peter Voorhees, Ray and Linda Terrill, Steve Oliver, Rick and Joni Costa, Chip and Corinne Mattingly, Glenn and Rita Eklund, Jeanette Roerig, Ned Seligman, Jeff Musgrave, Rand Hillier, Dan Batchelder, Mary Hind, Laborio and Terry Risorto, Michiel Shaw, Jeff and Bree Lair, Jim and Carol Wilson; Brad and Tess Moore; Pastor Dave Grisanti and his wife Debbie Grasanti; Pastor Russ and his wife Ina Reuther, Mahboob; Dutch Meyer; Havala Holmes and the Holmes family; Hans and Dorthey Ariens, Jenny Smith, the governments of Mexico, Thailand, Costa Rica; The Rotary Club; The United States Department of State; The United States Department of Defense; Focus on the Family, The National Ability Center and Meeche White; Rick Russo; Tito Bautista; Jose Manuel Castillo; Enrique Gonzales; Kimberly Perkins; Nuttha Suaysod, Bridgette Turner, Lois Collins, Skye Worthen and— others too numerous to list here. Special thanks to Jeff and Lisa Murphy. All photos taken by Lisa Murphy unless otherwise noted. They made this all possible. Website: mobilityproject.org

Thank you.

Preface

For over a decade, we helped to deliver mobility to the poorest of the poor all over the world. This is the story of our journey and the people we have served. From the hot deserts and mountains of Afghanistan to the jungles of Costa Rica and the beaches of Mexico, it has been one incredible adventure and life journey.

If we are wondering what our purpose is in life, read the stories of the brave people we helped to gain mobility. Once we find our path, our life journey becomes much easier. It does not mean there won't be difficulties. It just means we know where we are going and the importance of what we are doing. Our life path is better lit. It's when we don't know why we are here or where we are going that life can be trying and at times feel impossible.

Some of us became disabled as a result of illness, others via accident. Disability can happen for no particularly good reason. We have to adjust or give up. I was 21 and in world-class physical shape. It's called life.

We are often given Hobson choices of bad and worse. What will our adjustment be like in a world where wheelchairs encounter stairs at every turn and bathrooms are often not accessible? Now what?

Wheelchairs and disability are still relatively new to the modern world. For most of its history, the United States did not have laws mandating accessibility. When a place is wheelchair -accessible, doors are wide enough to enter, bathroom stalls are big enough to fit a wheelchair. Public places have ramps and curb cuts so a person on wheels can enter. These little things make a big difference to someone in a wheelchair.

But if you are not so fortunate as to live in a First World country, a major disability can be a death sentence. Many poor people who are disabled in developing countries either crawl on the ground, use a skate board or remain homebound.

One ignorant person had this to say about our delivery of wheelchairs to poor people in other countries. "What are you going to do that for? They are just going to die anyway." Yes, they are going to die anyway. We all are just going to die anyway. Our purpose in this life is to help each other on this journey.

We relieve some suffering by giving people a wheelchair, a walker or possibly just some crutches. Their lives immediately improve. After receiving a good wheelchair, they no longer crawl on the ground or are shut-ins in their homes. They have some mobility. Like Simon of antiquity, we help them carry their cross of disability. They in turn are very grateful.

After the wheelchair distributions, we go to the beach, shopping, deep sea fishing, to nice restaurants and enjoy the wonders and incredible beauty of our small planet. Humanitarian work is an adventure. Read along and join us in this adventure that took us all over the world helping the poorest of the poor.

Contents

Part One
Ability 1
   1. I Was Healthy. 2
   2. The Beginning. 11
   3. Jumping in Feet First: Nicaragua 17
   4. Networking and Growing. 23
   5. The Middle East: We Are Not a
      Christian Organization. 29

Part Two
A World Full Of Disabled. 39
   6. So Many Countries, So Little Time 40
   7. Traveling After 9/11 45
   8. Kabul. 59
   9. Costa Rica, the Most Beautiful Country on Earth. 67
  10. I Hate America and It's All Your Fault 80
  11. The Temples of Thailand 85

Part Three
The Future Of Disability. 96
  12. Then Came the CRASH. 97
  13. The World Access Project .101
  14. Mexico Is Not a Poor Country 104
  15. The Wheelchairs for Haiti Project 110
  16. Sao Tome- Slaves Were Processed Here. 114
  17. Rwanda Overcomes the Genocide 123
  18. Technology Gets Better and Better. 128
  19. There is Hope 133
  20. Serving the Lord Is a Gift .139

CONCLUSION. 166

Part One
ABILITY

Chapter One

I Was Healthy

"For the Spirit God gave us does not make us timid, but gives us power, love and self-discipline"

2 Timothy 1:7 NIV

Many people have good fortune, great health, siblings, two parents (both living), jobs, nice places to live and friends. That obviously was not my childhood and probably not yours. I don't know what sin I committed in my last life, but it must have been huge.

Maybe the Buddhists are right. Maybe our path in this life is the result of behaviors in a past life. Given the behavior of our Spanish and Roman ancestors, I can understand why I was being punished physically in this life. If it's bad, at one time or another it has happened to me. As I learned from our adventures traveling all over the world, all of us have to face adversity.

My smart, beautiful Spanish mother Amelia Blea Quintana died when I was not yet three. She was almost 26 years old. She was cheated out of a long, wonderful life. My father Conrado loved her with every fiber of his being. She died from complications while giving birth to what would have been her fourth child. The baby girl died too.

In my Spanish culture, when death takes a parent, the grandparents, aunts, uncles and other family members step up and raise the children. I was raised by my grandmother Ramoncita and my Tia Celsa in a small Spanish village in northern New Mexico. This dusty mountain town, Costilla, is about 50 miles north of Taos on the Colorado border. Nearby are the Sangre de Cristo Mountains. The village was built during the Spanish colonial era. The Spanish spoken in New Mexico is 16th century colonial Castilian, not the heavy Mexican Spanish or other dialects of 430 million people that share this beautiful language.

When my dad remarried, I moved from New Mexico to Tooele, Utah. I would go back home every summer right up until I went to college. My dad, Conrado Pelemon Quintana, was killed by a drunk driver when I was 10. I only knew him for two years. I have a few memories of him. He was physically strong, stocky and quiet. He was a soldier in World War II and a master carpenter. After the war, he led others from our small Spanish village in Northern New Mexico and moved to Tooele, Utah where there was work. He never got over the death of my mom. Seven years later, he married my Mormon stepmother, Wyona Adams.

When I was young, I was physically very strong from growing up on a small family farm and working out every day. I was a successful high school wrestler.

I walked onto the college wrestling team, then two weeks later I ended up in a wheelchair. I was 21 and had transverse myelitis, a neurological disorder that causes paralysis. I was angry. "Dear God, you took my parents, my grandparents and now you have taken my health? What the hell did I do to deserve a life on wheels?" It was not the result of violence or driving drunk, or doing something really stupid. It just happened. Damn it! It had to be divine punishment. Yup, if all else fails, blame God. See how far that will get you.

Before I give you the skinny on life on wheels, here is what my able-bodied life was like. My formative years were on that small subsistence farm in New Mexico. We did not have indoor plumbing or television. We were poor. We grew our own food and other than the money dad would mail us, we were so poor we could not afford to pay attention. So we worked from sun up until sundown.

Animals don't operate like a car or truck; you can't turn them off and take the keys indoors. These needy creatures demand food and water every day! We had to clean out their stinky stalls and pens. In return, we got to harvest them for food. Killing a pig is a big event. After you kill a pig, you have to clean it, gut it, skin it and cut the various parts up so you can cook and eat them. It is a lot of work.

Crops don't grow themselves. When it is your family's turn, you have to get up early to change the water from the culvert. If you don't water your crops, they won't grow. The nearest grocery store was 50 miles away. It would not have mattered if the store was close by. We did not have any money other than what my dad would send us from what was left over from his paycheck. We did get government powdered milk, eggs and horse meat. Our food choice was eat your beans, potatoes, corn and squash or go hungry. We never went hungry.

On a family farm, there is one child labor law: Children were born to provide the family with extra labor. No age is too young to work until you are exhausted. I remember the dust from the corn fields and the pumpkin patch with pumpkins that seemed to be as big as me. When you are five years old, the corn fields seemed to go on forever. We were not too young to help out. Young or old, you have a garden hoe, and go out to weed the corn fields, potatoes and beans. The whole family worked.

Everyone in our small Spanish village was poor. All my family members were in great physical shape. We walked everywhere, as did all of the villagers. Only a few families had vehicles. Spanish was the mother tongue and the Catholic Church provided spiritual guidance.

At night, Grandma Ramoncita would tell us these elaborate tales that always had a moral. My cousins and sisters would gather around and listen before prayers and much-needed sleep. If we had to pee during the night, there was a bedpan next to the bed. Every room had a cross or something to remind you of the church. The beauty of youth is that the fun-filled sunny days seem to last forever.

At school, we spoke English in class and Spanish everywhere else. The playground did not have grass and the dust seemed a normal part of growing up. Our clothes were often the hand-me-downs of an older sibling or cousin. I only recall one family having a phone.

Since we did not have indoor plumbing, at bath time we heated up water on the wood stove and put it in a large aluminum tub. Fortunately, I got to bathe before the girls. I can only imagine what it was like for the last girl to get in and bathe in much-used water.

My grandfather Fausto passed away at age 67 while I was still young. Fausto Quintana was a soldier in World War I. He had grey eyes, light skin and I never heard him speak one word in English. He was a quiet man who loved my grandmother Ramoncita. She had olive brown skin and beautiful green eyes.

My maternal grandparents, Flopida Martinez Blea and Andres Blea, lived in the next village. My sister Rosa was raised by them. Andres was a soldier in World War I. He was tall, strong and had iron discipline. Floripa was smart and had tremendous wisdom. I remember their funerals. I never heard either of them speak English.

Our village had electricity. We poached deer and elk from the mountains so we'd have meat. We caught fish in the nearby river. We were healthy.

Like children in villages all over the world, we did not know we were poor. We just knew we were loved and happy. After our chores, we would play in the river next to our homes. We would go for long hikes to the nearby plateau overlooking our small village. We would build playhouses in the field behind our farmhouse. We would play army in the woods by the pond filled with frogs and a few water snakes. We had fun. We had what we needed to enjoy life: good health, love and sunshine.

After my dad remarried I moved to Utah. We lived in a tiny white one-bedroom house. I slept on the couch. My stepmother Wyona Adams Quintana was very pregnant with my little brother Steve.

Our house was next to some apartments where my cousin Eli lived. He had just arrived from the old country. He lived with his mother Maxine, his father Eli and his little brother Randy. We were inseparable, playing together constantly. Both of us had the misfortune to be bit on the ass by an angry German shepherd who obviously did not like Spanish children. I still hate that breed of dog.

It was the '60s. The Vietnam War was in full force. There were race riots after Martin Luther King was assassinated. This was the height of the Cold War. When I was able-bodied, I had a photographic memory. I tried to figure it all out.

In 1969, Neil Armstrong landed on the moon while the Vietnam War was raging and the streets of America were exploding with riots. George Wallace was preaching states rights. It was crystal clear that hatred of people of color was going to continue. Like every child my age, I wanted to be an astronaut. The space program was intriguing. But I don't recall ever seeing any non-white pilots or women astronauts. This was my youth. Astronauts were male and white.

By the time I got to high school, I had made friends with my cousins the Martinez boys, who lived down the street, and with a few neighborhood kids. I would get on my bike and tell them, "We are going on a bike ride up to Middle Canyon." Or I would get my baseball glove and ball. "We are going to play baseball." Other times I would tell my friends, "Today we are going to play football."

I played high school football. Our team sucked. On second thought, we were not quite that good. I weighed 120 pounds and played cornerback, running back and third-string quarterback. Basic physics will tell you that an object in motion will continue in motion until a force of equal or greater force changes its direction.

A 240-pound running back was coming in my direction. I went to tackle him. He hit me. I went flying and was lying flat on my back. The huge running back stepped on my chest as he ran for a touchdown! I looked up at the sky. "I suck at this game."

On weekends, I raced motorcycles in the west desert. I would parachute with a group of teenagers who had to try out this adventure. The parachute outfit was run out of town when a young lady our age was killed. Her chute did not open.

I was constantly in the mountains hiking the many trails. In the fall, I would go deer hunting with my friends, Victor Graham and Richard Sandoval. They were part of the many Spanish Catholic families in Tooele from Taos, New Mexico.

I used my dad's old 32 caliber rifle. We would hike until our feet and legs were tired. One time I was hunting with my little brother Steve. He is eight years younger. I forgot that our family rifle shot low and to the left. A buck was on the trail in shooting range. I aimed right at him. BOOM, low and to the left. The buck took off running.

The next day I asked Steve to go hunting with me. He declined. Steve was a mischievous little guy. He hit this kid right in the head with a snowball and knocked him off his bike. The poor child fell in a cold pool of water. The kid came after him. Being his big brother, I beat up the poor kid.

The '60s and '70s were a different era. Our country was one very racist place. The local white kids hated us but they were lousy fighters. One punch to the nose and they would take off.

I don't have fear like normal people. It did not matter. My memories of growing up in Tooele, Utah are almost all bad. My Spanish friends were thrown out of school, mostly for fighting. The white kids were not punished as severely for the same conduct. The names I was called left an imprint for life.

I had no plans to stay there. College and law school were in my future. Life after high school was one big adventure of riding motorcycles, drinking beer and having a blast. But from the time I was young, there was always something wrong physically. Despite being in phenomenal physical condition, my body always tingled.

Regardless of how much I worked out, my entire body always felt like it was on fire. I saw doctor after doctor. They had no idea what was going on.

Martha, the mother of my child, was a very pretty, quiet lady who is smart but grew up poor, almost destitute. I fell madly in love with her. She had a perfect figure, long brown hair and an attitude. Given a better home environment, she could have graduated from any college in the nation.

I was in college. My hair was long. I played tennis with my friends and hung out with them when I was not working or studying. Luckily, I had enough scholarships and money to pay for school. Life was good. I had roommates from France and Iran. My French roommate Christian was studying chemical engineering. He was brilliant and we instantly hit it off. He taught me how to drink red wine.

My roommate Mansoor was this terrific Persian guy. He was going to study medicine. When he learned that I was not a spy for Savak, the Iranian secret police, we became friends. He explained that you could not just overthrow the Shah. The institutions would just install a new Shah. The Shah was at that time the worst violator of human rights on the planet. The United States installed him and he terrorized Iran.

There was a whiny kid from Saudi Arabia that shared our dorm. He kept accusing me of stealing his stereo. I told him I had my own things and I did not steal. I also told him that if he accused me of stealing again I was going to work him over. He accused me and I picked him up, threw him against the wall, and punched him in the belly. He started crying. So I let him go. Growing up, my Spanish friends would try to beat me up for free.

My back always felt like it was on fire. One day the burning in my nerves just exploded. I kept falling down. Martha and I were living together in student housing. She was very pregnant and I was very ambitious. I went to the doctor. He could not figure out what was wrong. The pain was excruciating.

It was early evening and I collapsed. I had to crawl everywhere and I could not pee as my insides no longer worked. I needed help. I lost my job. It was almost one week of crawling on the floor before we realized I was not getting better. We sought help.

I had seen the many advertisements of the Multiple Sclerosis Society asking for donations. I looked up their phone number in the Yellow Pages and called them as I was laying on the floor.

"I don't know what is wrong but do you have a wheelchair I can borrow? I am really sick and can't walk. I will return it when I get better."

The person at the other end was smug. "We will rent you one."

"No, you don't understand. I don't have any money. I am a college student. I have become sick with God knows what and I need to use a wheelchair until I get better. I have lost my job and I am not going to be able to wrestle again until I recover from whatever has made me not walk."

His reply remained, "We will rent you one."

"Look, you don't understand. I don't have any money. I am sick and in college. I have lost my job, I need a wheelchair."

I can just see him laughing, "Well, we will rent you one."

What part of 'I don't have any money' do you not understand? What do you guys do with all of the millions of dollars you raise?"

"We raise public awareness of neurological problems."

I was having one.

Martha went to the University of Utah Hospital and "borrowed" a wheelchair so I could get around. I seriously doubt they noticed. There were unoccupied wheelchairs everywhere at that hospital. She had to drive me around as I could no longer use my legs and was in horrific pain.

The doctors thought I was mentally ill. If you can't figure out what is physically wrong, send the patient to a shrink. They put me in the psych ward. When the phone would ring, I would pick it up. "Funny farm, patient speaking." A doctor kept observing my behavior and concluded that I was not mentally ill. I was transferred to a different unit where people were there with broken necks from rodeo or football, car accidents, falls and more.

One kid had both his arms cut off from a work electrocution. A lady was struggling to stand from the nerve damage of multiple sclerosis. Other people had severe brain injuries.

One young lady was there because her dad threw all of the children off a hotel roof under the delusion his deity had ordered it. She had numerous broken bones and what appeared to be brain damage. All of her siblings died, as did her parents.

There were people in comas. Name the disability, the hospital and the doctors were trying to fix broken bodies. Nature had other plans. Eventually, I was able to walk with crutches and braces. The braces cut into my legs and at the end of each day, I was exhausted. But I had a lot to live for. I had a woman I loved and a child.

The best day of my life was when my son was born. I was six months into disability, in a wheelchair and as I went to my little student apartment, the name Isaac was written on my ramp. I have always been a fan of Isaac Newton and Alexander the Great so I named him Isaac Alexander Quintana.

My first day of law school, I ran into a wrestling buddy from college. Instead of saying hello, he took one look at me on my crutches and asked, "What the hell happened to you?" I made it through law school on crutches and walked for about twenty years. One day my neurological problems got worse. I no longer walk. Now I use a wheelchair all the time. I still use my exercise bike to keep my legs from atrophying. I never fully recovered and I can tell I am slowly getting worse.

When I first got partially paralyzed, I could no longer wrestle, box, race my motorcycle in the desert, hike up in the mountains and do numerous other activities I once enjoyed. Young marriages seldom survive and soon I was a divorced attorney, raising my son and my nephews John and Jimmy. I still enjoyed life.

I could still play tennis. I took up wheelchair tennis because sport has always been part of my life. I used to box and take karate. I like hitting things. I played tennis with my friends, as I did not have the time or money to travel to wheelchair tennis tournaments. I worked full-time as a single dad and an attorney. In time, I made enough money practicing law that I was able to travel and play in national wheelchair tennis tournaments. That was 1994. I was 17 years into disability world.

Fast forward to 2004 and I am at a wheelchair tennis tournament in Truckee, California, with my long-time friend Richard St. Denis. We were playing tennis. I had just finished getting my second divorce.

Richard asked me to go on a wheelchair distribution and sports camp to Mazatlan, Mexico. That distribution was with the Mobility Project, a non-profit organization that delivered wheelchairs all over the world. That trip led me on a journey of adventure with my friends, Lisa and Jeff Murphy, Richard St. Denis and others that would become my new life.

Everyone on the planet is on a different path. If we are willing to listen to the Lord, we will find our purpose in life. This is how my friends Lisa and Jeff were led on a path that has taken them all over the world.

Chapter Two

The Beginning

How Lisa and Jeff Murphy started
delivering wheelchairs all over the world

"And we know that in all things God works for the good of those who love him, who have been called according to his purpose.

Romans 8:25 NIV

November 1998. A deadly hurricane hit the Atlantic coast, causing more than 19,000 fatalities in Central America. My husband Jeff and I had a heart to serve the disabled poor in other countries. We had visited Mexico on our 20th anniversary and saw that there were individuals begging on the streets. They were actually crawling on the ground due to their disabilities. We tried to purchase a wheelchair in Cabo San Lucas, Mexico. We could not find any, not one. This was not even a possibility.

Jeff is a certified Assistive Technology Professional, which is a fancy way to say that he fits people in wheelchairs. He is a seating specialist. When we saw people crawling on the ground needing wheelchairs, we were very concerned and surprised, knowing that thousands of wheelchairs in the United States end up in landfills.

We came back from our trip and shared our story with our Bible study group. We told them we really need to do something about this. We prayed about this desire to help for the next year. Then things began to happen which led us all over the world.

We went on a youth mission trip to Baja with our youth pastor's small group. We brought a few wheelchairs for distribution to the many poor disabled we had seen on previous trips. This was very rewarding. The people receiving the wheelchairs and their families were very grateful. A few months later, our pastor was going on his annual humanitarian mission trip to Bulgaria. Jeff and I wanted to go. A small group of maybe three or four volunteers were going. Jeff had provided each member with a wheelchair to give away either to a church, hospital or an individual in need. Dave Grisanti, our pastor, was aware of the shortages of durable medical supplies as well as wheelchairs from his previous trips.

As soon as we returned from Mexico, Jeff started dumpster diving at nursing homes, hospitals and other places to gather wheelchairs for distribution abroad. After a while, these institutions started giving us wheelchairs rather than throwing them away.

The trip to Bulgaria was very expensive. Still, we told Dave, we would love to go. I remember him standing before our church congregation and asking for support. He told us who was going and said what the volunteers would be doing. The main plan was that the group would be speaking and sharing at churches.

Then Dave told the congregation Jeff and I wanted to go with them. Our church planned to deliver some wheelchairs to perhaps a hospital facility that was in need. He asked the congregation to please support Jeff. He was needed to do the proper seating of the disabled. Fitting someone in a wheelchair is like finding the right shoes. They need to be fit just right, not too big, too wide, too heavy or too small.

I was disappointed. I felt as if I had no purpose, nothing to offer. I felt as if God had told me "You, Lisa are not going anywhere." This had become such a passion and almost obsession with us. We knew in our hearts that this was our purpose. It was like nothing we had felt before. This was a big deal. In our experience, this is how God works.

About a month before, Dave had gone to a church conference where he heard a missionary explain their humanitarian mission. He worked with a group called Hope Haven ministries. They collected the used wheelchairs that were being thrown out. They too, could be called "dumpster divers," so to speak.

Then the wheelchairs were repaired by prison inmates in Iowa. After the repaired wheelchairs were in usable condition, they were shipped by container to different parts of the world. We could not believe it. We called them right away. They told us "Oh, you do not understand what we do." Steve Oliver and Ray Terrill, co-founders of the Mobility Project, said that "we do very specialized seating for individuals. As a matter of fact, we have about 200 pediatric wheelchairs on their way to Nicaragua as we speak."

They said, "We need a professional, someone who has been trained in the field." We then said that is what Jeff does, he is a seating specialist. They replied, "Oh my goodness, we have been praying for someone just like you!" They asked us to go with them to Nicaragua. We were very saddened and had to say no. We could not afford it. Jeff was going to Bulgaria. We could not get time off work even if we did have the funds.

Jeff was able to go to Bulgaria because he was rear-ended in his vehicle and the insurance paid exactly the amount of the plane ticket, $905.00. This was received in the mail the day of the deadline. Coincidence, some might say. But we knew the Lord was in charge, it certainly was not us. Obviously, his vehicle remained dented for quite a while. It was merely cosmetic.

Hurricane Mitch hit Central America while Jeff was in Bulgaria. It was all over the news. I called Steve and Ray and offered any medical supplies they might need to take with them.

Since Jeff was in the durable medical equipment line of work, he could get hold of medical supplies such as wound care packages, bandages, etc. Like wheelchairs, medical supplies in the United States are thrown away despite being still usable. Jeff started collecting medical supplies as soon as we returned from Mexico. He could get many things donated from vendors, hospitals and therapy facilities. We just needed to get these donated items to Colorado. That is where the "Mobility Project" was based.

At that time, we lived in Seattle, Washington. Steve and Ray were upset as the volunteers who had signed up for the distribution backed out due to the danger from flooding. People in the destructive path of the hurricane were dying due to infection after the tragedy. There were not enough volunteers and medical supplies to go around. Steve and Ray asked us to please reconsider. They desperately needed our help.

They could not complete the wheelchair distribution by themselves. They had only completed one distribution previously with the help of Hope Haven and their volunteers. Hope Haven had the experience needed for a distribution to be successful. I explained to them that Jeff was in Bulgaria. The Mobility Project team was leaving for Nicaragua a week after Jeff returned from Bulgaria. As usual, there was the money thing — or rather lack of it. This has been a problem the entire time we delivered wheelchairs all over the world.

They insisted that we pray about it, perhaps discuss it with Pastor Dave, and get back to them. I talked to Jeff that evening. Of course, he wanted to go. Dave was very conservative. He advised against the trip, but we still felt we had to go. The draw was indescribable, a calling if you will. It was like God was personally asking us to help his poor and disabled.

I spoke to our children about the trip. Our two eldest children, Shawna and Ryan, also wanted to go. It was one of those many tragedies that you hear about on the news and feel helpless. Here we were, given an opportunity to make a difference. We all felt drawn to the calling. Then the most amazing thing happened.

I was at a Bible study at the home of Russ Reuther our assistant pastor. He asked me to share the story with the group. He knew about it because I had shared the story with him a few days before while Jeff was still out of the country. I was seeking advice. We were good friends and he understood a "calling". He did not want to go against the pastor of our church, but he felt we should ask the congregation on Sunday if they wanted to help.

After the meeting, a woman that I had never really met before asked to speak to me privately. She wanted to help. She said after we asked the congregation on Sunday for the funds to please let her know how much money was donated, then let her know how much we needed. She would make up the difference.

I said this could be thousands of dollars! She said calmly, "Yes, I know." She said that immediately on hearing the story, God told her this was right. I broke down and cried. I knew this was not a coincidence, a lucky break or selfish whim to get our way. This was meant to be. Once again, the Lord was in charge.

We found through our time in the ministry that people love to give money for things they believe in. Some would remark that they could never do anything like this themselves, but they could give money to help make it happen. This was a beautiful picture of Christians working together to accomplish God's work. We had no money but every desire to do the work. We always felt sharing the word with people was good but showing how God was working through us was much more powerful.

Jeff and I are very strong in our faith in the Lord. Our testimony is very strong because of the Lord saving our lives. Ten years earlier we were involved in the crystal meth craze. We were not hanging out with drug addicts. It just happened, it evolved. Jeff had never touched a drug his whole life. Some of us smoked marijuana now and then. Jeff hated it. But he tried cocaine one time and that was it. He found his drug of choice. Cocaine led to stronger demons, more evil things.

We lived in Arizona at the time. We got deep into drugs and involved with very dangerous people. Meth is the devil. It took the best man I ever met and turned him into a completely different person. We fought all the time and could not survive without the drug. Our children were 10, 8 and 5 years of age. After a couple of years, I fell apart and wanted our lives back. I then did the one thing Jeff was afraid of. I went to our parents for help. That night Jeff was really distraught. For our parents to even imagine that we were doing illegal drugs was not something either of us could face.

His shame was deadly. We got through that night and I started seeing a counselor right away. Jeff went a couple of times but he was not on the same page. We were so deep into this lifestyle that drugs were dropped off at our house whether we wanted them or not.

Jesus was right. "The lust for money is truly the root of all evil." The temptation from the money and effect of the drugs was too great.

During a counseling session, Jeff got very sarcastic with the counselor and walked out. She asked to speak to me after he left. I respected her a great deal. She was a recovering heroin addict before she became a counselor. I knew she understood the illness we were dealing with. She began to explain to me that Jeff might not make it and I had a choice to make.

She said that only about 10 percent of couples that go through this are successful. She said that I would probably have to leave him to get sober. I started crying uncontrollably. I told her that I loved this man more than life itself. I met him when I was 15 years old and loved him ever since. I said that I would feel like I was leaving him to die alone in a burning building.

She took my shoulders in her hands and made me sit down, looked straight into my eyes and said "Think about this. You are leaving that burning building with your children in your arms." I finally got it. I went home and told my 10-year-old daughter to pack her things. She had to help her brothers because we had to leave daddy so he could get better.

Jeff returned home while we were packing. He begged us to stay. He was very emotional when I told him I would take the children to my mom's and come back to speak with him. But he knew this was it. There was no turning back and nothing would ever be the same again. When I returned, he was crying. I asked him what was wrong and why didn't he understand that our children's lives were at stake? He said,

"I do understand. I said a prayer to God and he showed me the person I have become and I cannot bear it." He was completely stripped of his prior life and was a mere shred of himself. He was helpless. This is where he needed to be to be able to save himself.

The police were watching us. We were worried about having drugs planted on us as we were finally drug-free. Our love for each other, our family and the Lord saved us from ourselves. While Jeff was alone, he prayed, "Please, God, get us out of this." He heard a voice: "Leave, get your family and leave right now."

We packed up some of our belongings into a 1956 trailer from a sand pit my dad found and gave us. We signed our house over to Jeff's dad and left our children with my parents. It was a monsoon that night. Jeff's father drove our car out of town. We drove his father's car so we could leave the county unnoticed in a torrential rain. We drove all night to Washington state. We were listening to the radio and a song by Bon Jovi was playing, "Living on a Prayer." I looked at Jeff and asked, "have you ever listened to the words of this song?" "No, not really." And this song described exactly what we were doing. The old truck had holes in the floorboard. We left with $200.00. We prayed and God was directing us. "God has the answer for us." We were about halfway and the song described our situation. "You live for the fight when that's all you got."

When we got there, we lived on Jeff's sister's property in the trailer. We prayed and the Lord answered our prayers. We were safely out of the dangerous drug world and never went back.

We started our lives all over again. Within about three months, we were able to get an apartment. Soon my parents drove our children back to us. This was one of the best times in our lives. We had few possessions, but we had each other. This is when God began his work in us. The Lord saved us from drugs. Now we were called to do something wonderful that would change the lives of thousands of disabled poor people all over the world.

Chapter Three

Jumping in Feet First: Nicaragua

"Ask and it will be given to you; seek and you will find; knock and the door will be opened to you."

Mathew 7:7 NIV

Jinotepe Nicaragua

The Creator gives us free agency. Animals cannot choose between right and wrong. They do their job. They entertain the Creator. The reality is, most things in life are clearly beyond our control. When Jeff and Lisa decided to serve the Lord, their entire lives turned around.

They replaced something as powerful as illegal drugs with the love of God. Lisa explains what happened next:

After what we had been through in our previous drug-using lives and with over 10 years of sobriety, jumping on a plane to a country we had never been and meeting people we had never seen face to face was not a stretch for us. It was an exciting mission to the unknown. We welcomed it with open arms. It felt right.

A week after Jeff returned from Bulgaria, we were on the plane to Managua, Nicaragua. All we had was the sheer faith that we were doing the right thing. Nothing ever felt so right my whole life except marrying Jeff when I was 18 years old.

Pastor Dave was still not on board with our journey. He advised against it and we went anyway. He was a worrywart. We had a clear vision that God had put it on our hearts. Jeff, our two oldest children (who were 20 and 17 at the time) and a good friend from church, Nate, went on this distribution. It was all funded by the amazing people in our congregation. They paid for our airfare and passports.

We did not know the people we were meeting in Nicaragua. There was no internet and no social media. We got off the plane and they found us right away, as the airport was tiny. It looked more like a warehouse than an airport. Our connection with the Nicaraguan team was incredible.

We got along like we knew each other our whole lives. We had the same goals in mind and connected spiritually. We shared the same passion for the disabled poor. Prior to this trip, our Nicaraguan team had only completed one distribution. They were really looking for the expertise that Jeff brought. We were excited to be there and just wanted to get working right away. There was a problem, though — one that happened many times in this line of work.

Customs had not released the chairs yet, so we waited. This happens a lot in the Third World. Customs wanted a bribe. We never paid them. If we paid the bribe Customs would always hold our goods. We would have to pay a bribe everywhere we went.

We had a couple of days, so we took a plane to the Caribbean side of Nicaragua to a village called Puerto Cabezas. There were no roads through the jungle from the capital that led to the village. We took a prop plane and landed on a dirt road in the town. This was where the founder, Steve Oliver, served as a missionary a few years back. This is where he had the first distribution. He met a woman named Martha who was quadriplegic. She was born and raised in the village.

Martha was amazing. Here is where Steve discovered the needs of the disabled that existed everywhere in the Third World. The village was tiny with dirt roads, small huts and a few buildings, no indoor plumbing or television. As you can imagine, the wheelchairs that had been delivered were in poor shape due to the harsh conditions. However, despite these harsh living conditions, poor dirt roads, no sidewalks or curb cuts, these people were now at least mobile. Prior to getting a wheelchair, they either crawled or were carried.

The village was devastated by the hurricane. There was plenty to do. Steve had taken some wheelchairs to them before with Hope Haven. The villagers had built a small workshop. We brought all kinds of parts, cushions, catheters and medical supplies. Then we helped with the cleanup from the hurricane. We cleaned the workshop and repaired the wheelchairs they had on hand. Families came from all over the village to welcome us and to get their wheelchairs repaired.

We were told that one reason there were so many disabled was due to the bends — decompression sickness. Of course, like most Third World countries, education and the right equipment is always lacking. In order to provide for their families, they would use old scuba gear to dive to the bottom of the ocean for the coveted shellfish of the region. This was their main industry.

If you are not educated on the risks of ascending too quickly from a dive, you get the bends and its painful, lasting effects. In the developed world, there is treatment for the bends. We use a hyperbaric chamber. These people did not have access to a doctor, let alone that kind of expensive decompression equipment. This disability is a very common occurrence in this part of the world.

Jeff is an amazing mechanic and also gifted with people skills. I always said that when Jeff was a restaurant manager he could fire an employee and they would thank him for it. He has such a genuine heart and everyone who meets him feels it, too. This is one of the reasons why I fell in love with him. I have always admired that particular trait and I remain in awe of it to this day.

While we were working in the shop, everyone in the group was sure that we were going to have to throw away many of the wheelchairs because they were in such bad shape. Jeff directed all of us and he was able to salvage wheelchairs from what people here in the states would call garbage. Everyone thought it was almost magical. We knew it was God. I have always thought from that moment on that if you show up for God, He will show up to help you. The Lord has continued throughout the years to come through for us time and time again. We were never left on our own.

Jeff was able to help some people with open wounds, commonly known as pressure sores. This became part of our ministry. He was quite passionate about it from learning anatomy here in the states. Without wound treatment, people can get infections and die quickly, especially in a moist climate like Nicaragua. Whether you are in a poor or rich country, infections can spread fast throughout the body.

People with injuries and no feeling in parts of their bodies due to paralysis can have an open wound and not be aware of their injury. These pressure sores or ulcers are one of the biggest threats to a person in a wheelchair who has no sensation. Jeff studied the wound treatment techniques used by Dr. David Warner, who wrote "Where There Is No Doctor." These techniques are used all over the world and many lives have been saved. His book is on the shelves of many poor clinics all over the developing world.

I often wondered why God chose me for this calling as I did not believe I had much to contribute. But, what we believe of our abilities differs from what God knows we are capable of doing. In retrospect, I am a good organizer. I did not realize how important that was at the time. I thought the glory was in the giving of the wheelchairs and treating the wounds. But wheelchair distributions cannot be done without organizing and a competent team effort.

After some rewarding days of working to clean up from the destruction of the hurricane, we received word that the wheelchairs were going to be released. Customs gave up on their bribe. We would be able to bless 200 children with specialized wheelchairs. Yes, 200. Unfortunately, we only had a couple of days to do this as we were booked to fly home in a few days. We were all so excited. I will never forget this distribution.

We had not eaten much and lived on the protein bars we brought with us. Supplies were low in country after this devastating hurricane. We were all tired from the long, hard days and uncomfortable sleeping arrangements that came with the rough territory. The excitement and our faith that we were doing the right thing kept us going.

After we loaded the semi-truck with the wheelchairs, we drove up to Jinotep, a small village in the mountains. While the village was small, there were about 45,000 people in the surrounding territory. It seemed small because there was no development as we know it here: no fast food drive-ups, grocery stores and no "chain stores" of any kind. There were tiny cardboard houses, little tiendas, in people's homes. They sold items locally farmed, milk, homemade breads and the occasional bottled Coke drink, which we found was everywhere in the world.

It was overwhelming to see all the wheelchairs arrive on a flatbed truck. They were all tangled, as they had been tied down and packed tightly to survive the bumpy ride to this remote jungle village. These were very specialized chairs donated from a U.S. company that was going out of business.

New, these wheelchairs would range from $2,000 to $5,000 at their manufacturer's suggested retail price. What a gift! These specialized wheelchairs had all sorts of seating options. They were very adjustable and made for children with extreme disabilities. Jeff knew exactly what to do with them. The Mobility Project founders, Steve and Ray, were amazed and ready to learn from him.

I was excited but nervous when all the people started to show up. There were over 100 people with disabilities with their families. I was told to get a picture of every chair and recipient and to have them fill out some paperwork. I was a bit overwhelmed until my organization skills kicked in. Then my daughter Shawna and I had everything set up. We helped as we could while we were waiting to get the disabled people in wheelchairs.

Some people were dragged in on pieces of wood, blankets, and wheelbarrows. The smaller children were carried to the distribution. I saw a mother with a little girl in her arms shifting from side to side. The mom was tired. There was no telling how far the baby was carried. I was drawn to the long line. It was hot outside, as this is the tropics. I realized we needed to do something to make them more comfortable.

I went to the mom and asked in my very broken Spanish if I could hold her little girl so she could rest. The little girl started crying. The mother handed her to me. She was beautiful, about 3 to 4 years old with spina bifida, a birth defect where there is incomplete closing of the backbone and membranes around the spinal cord. This birth defect leaves people partially paralyzed. The child was also blind.

We seemed to understand each other perfectly. She said that God had sent us and she was very thankful. I knew at that moment God was telling me to just love his people. No skills are required for love, only your heart. I started crying. The rest of the day was the best Thanksgiving we had ever had. We ate only protein bars and never felt so content. I knew we were right where we were supposed to be. The whole group felt the same. We were very hopeful of what was yet to come.

After this distribution, our faith and our mission took us all over the world. When the Lord gets you out of a difficult situation, be thankful and humbly serve. Your life will never be the same. After the first trip to Nicaragua, we continued our Christian work and went on to visit almost every poor country on the planet, more than 50 distributions to more than 20 countries over 14 years. We went to some countries many times as their need is so great.

Chapter Four

Networking and Growing

"For it is by grace you have been saved, through faith—and this is not from yourselves, it is the gift of God— not by works, so that no one can boast. For we are God's workmanship, created in Christ Jesus to do good works, which God prepared in advance for us to do."

Ephesians 2:8-10 NIV

People often asked how we got the word out about delivering wheelchairs to the disabled poor all over the world. It was all word of mouth. As technology improved, eventually we had our website.

We would share the word with churches, Rotary clubs, Lions clubs, anywhere with any group wanting to help that would have us. Steve Oliver and I would do most of the public presentations. I used to begin my talks by saying that my husband Jeff did all the hard work. I took pictures and talked about it. This would always get a laugh because as everyone understands, it takes a village.

I was the administrator and was one part of the organization and I recognized that my work was important. *"The body is a unit, though it is made up of many parts; and though all its parts are many, they form one body"* 1 Corinthians 12:12

Jeff was the seating specialist and our volunteers provided hands-on labor. I began working from home full-time. I was making several trips to Colorado every couple of months to meet with the Mobility Project staff and coordinate global wheelchair distributions. We averaged about four distributions a year and sometimes more. We would be out of the country for about two weeks at a time. We had most of our board meetings in the field at distribution sites.

We often took up to 20 volunteers per trip. Everyone involved did the recruiting. This was the easy part until we started going to the Middle East. The distribution in Nicaragua was so chaotic Jeff and I were determined to make it much better organized — and we did.

We both worked in restaurants and knew how to organize people and work schedules. We were certainly not the first organization to do wheelchair distributions to poor countries. Joni Eareckson Tada is the pioneer in this field. Her wonderful organization is called Joni and Friends. I took the time and learned everything I could about her. She had a very popular Christian radio show out of California. Joni is a quadriplegic and has devoted her life to serving the Lord. She is amazing.

There was a movie written about her in the '70s called "The Other Side of the Mountain." Mark Richard of Hope Haven had worked with her. Mark's brother David also had a group out of California that did wheelchair distributions. They paved a path and we created some of our own roads.

We raised all the funds for the Mobility Project ourselves. This was brutal. We got a few grants, had yearly fundraising events and sent out a quarterly newsletter. It was a joy to write about our time in the field and share with all our supporters the names and faces of the people that benefited from their direct support. Donors loved the pictures of the many people they helped with their generosity.

When we first started traveling, our youngest son Aaron resented the Mobility Project. It was time-consuming and took us away from him. To cure this, we knew we had to bring him with us on a distribution and get him involved.

We were going to Guatemala for a summit for medical ministries from all over the world. This was a great chance to learn from each other and network. We were going to have classes and do a wheelchair distribution. Aaron was a very active 16-year old who loved baseball and all sports. He is an outstanding athlete and physically strong like his dad. Like many teenagers who know everything, he thought what we were doing was ... well, embarrassing and yes ... weird. That changed over time as he realized the importance of what we were doing and became involved in helping others.

We would speak at church often. And we were spoken of at church all the time. This made it quite difficult to get him through the church door at times. We tried everything to get Aaron to come with us. Nothing was working. One of our regular supporters actually offered to sponsor his trip — this being another small miracle in the hundreds we experienced on our life journey. Our church sponsors were so in tune with our needs. It was incredible. I remember being so upset that Aaron did not want to go with us that I was crying in our dining room. We had purchased the ticket for him already but he was really dug in.

I dreaded even the thought of forcing him to get on the airplane. He came into the room and told me he was sorry but he just hated the thought of going. Then God gave me the words to explain to him. His love was baseball. I asked him to think about how much he loved the game. I asked him to think about how he felt when he hit the ball and he knew it was going over the fence. I also asked him how good it felt when he looked out to the stands and saw that I was there and his dad had made it to the game. What a bonus for both of us to be there because this was rare, as Jeff was constantly working. I told him this is how we feel when we are in the field doing what the Lord has called us to do. For us to share our gift with him was our greatest wish. He looked at me and said, "Okay, Mom. I will go."

Yes, God had a plan for sure. The summit in Guatemala is where we met Richard St. Denis. Richard is in a wheelchair from a skiing accident in 1976. He is a topnotch athlete. He was delivering wheelchairs to Mexico and driving them down himself from his home in Colorado.

We all had a wonderful time together. Aaron got to play wheelchair basketball and tried other sports as well. He worked with Richard most of the time. Richard joined the Mobility Project and we added wheelchair sports to our distributions. This set us apart from all the other ministries and made us very unique. We not only provided mobility, hope, dignity and independence, but we were able to show them how to use their new gift. Thereafter, sports and training on how to use a wheelchair was something that was incorporated into every distribution. Sometimes we had to get familiar with a country before bringing Rich. When we went to the Middle East, we did one the most epic sports camps in the infamous stadium in Kabul, Afghanistan.

Richard had a timeshare at a hotel in Mazatlán, Mexico. He had worked out an arrangement with the hotel to hold a sports camp in December for the disabled locals in the area. He worked with DIF, the local Mexican government office of disabilities. DIF is a Mexican government public assistance agency that works to strengthen families. They do a good job with limited resources. DIF arranged for transportation to the hotel and back for the annual four-day sporting event for people with disabilities.

Rich would end the sports camp with a tennis tournament for all disabled athletes. He would talk with U.S. wheelchair tennis players throughout the year at various tennis tournaments. Then he would ask

American players to donate their old sport chairs. After the sports camp, Rich would take the sports chairs to Mazatlán and give them to disabled athletes. It was always an incredible event.

Rich would also get gifted U.S. tennis players to go to Mazatlán and volunteer their services for the camp. The hotel let all the volunteers stay for free during the sports camp. This was our cushiest outreach yet and the one trip we were never short on volunteers. We would tell our volunteers they should do a rough outreach first to earn this one because it was so nice. Richard and his lovely ex-wife Hazuki are very smart and love Mexico.

After Richard started working with us, we were able to take wheelchair distributions to the next level. We would collect sport chairs throughout the year and send them to Mexico in a container with other specialty chairs, combining the sport outreach with a local distribution. Aaron participated in every Mazatlán outreach we did before he moved to Hawaii. Aaron also went with me on a survey trip to Peru. After Aaron was on his own, he appreciated what we did and the work that went into a distribution. This changed his outlook on life.

Mazatlán is where we met our good friend Danny Quintana. I think Jeff picked him up at the airport. They instantly hit it off and to this day he is one of our closest friends. Although Danny missed the first part of our distribution activity, after 2004 he went with us all over the world.

Eventually, we were collecting wheelchairs in Colorado and Washington state. We would store them for Hope Haven ministries. They would pick them up and refurbish them. The containers were then shipped from Iowa. Sometimes we would step into a country for Hope Haven. They had so much going on in the world they did not have enough staff to complete all the distributions themselves.

By the year 2003, we had moved the main office to our home in Washington. Ray would step away from the ministry a couple of years later and Steve Oliver moved to Mexico with his new wife Meriam, who he met in Mazatlán. We collected many wheelchairs and traveled all over the state promoting the ministry.

I would sometimes go with him and do presentations. We had many therapists volunteer as it was such a perfect match. Therapists contributed so much on the trips. All the nursing homes would have Jeff go into their storage units and clean them out. He would fix what the nursing homes could use. They would give him the rest. It was not long until we were refurbishing all our own chairs and shipping them from Seattle.

During this time, I had an intern named Alex Rice who moved from Colorado to help us. She became one of our closest friends. She now has an outreach mission in Colorado. She helps Afghan women and children. She has the biggest heart of anyone I know. We love her dearly.

Steve Oliver was still the president and I was promoted to vice-president. The administration part got to be so much that we brought on Jenny Smith from Kentucky and Brock Moller, a good friend from our church. Both traveled all over the world with us. Jenny became a quadriplegic at age 17 as a result of a gymnastics accident. She did a somersault, hit hard and broke her neck. The fickle hand of fate had her become part of wheelchair world.

Jenny is one of the mentally strongest people I have ever met. She challenged me to be a better person. She never complains and always has a positive attitude despite her difficult physical situation. She challenged everyone who met her along the way. Jenny has many computer skills and helped me with things like operating manuals and grants, etc. Her eye for details is amazing. Jenny is very smart. She speaks Spanish and also learned Dari. Afghanistan stole her heart.

Brock Moller brought his great work ethic as a volunteer and helped with fundraising and numerous other tasks. It's like the Lord would bring us the right players to fit missing needs. Brock has amazing computer and people skills. He is one of the hardest workers we ever had volunteer. He picked up wheelchairs, refurbished them, ran the warehouse, raised volunteers and helped to load many containers for us. Brock was just fun to have around with his constant smile and great attitude. It is easier to accomplish something difficult when the people around you are in good spirits.

Jim and Carol Wilson knew Steve and soon became involved. Jim wanted to help and soon he and Carol were traveling with us all over the world. Jim is a hotrod builder and is one of the best mechanics we ever had work with us. He would usually man one of the distribution stations. He would always be helping the other stations with fixing wheelchairs and whatever needed to be adjusted. He could figure out how to make tools or parts if something was missing.

Carol would help with the administration, cleanup, the work crews, whatever was needed. They also helped where they could in raising money. At times, some of their family members or friends would go with them. We called them the A Team. There were some people you just had to have on a wheelchair distribution. There were about 300 in our church and about 80 percent of them at one time or another were involved in a distribution with us. It was touching that they cared and helped out. These youth ministries provided great guidance for young people.

We were in church one day and Jeff and I were looking at each other. Everyone in the room at some of our meetings had gone on these humanitarian missions.

Mary, a humble, successful wealthy woman who likes to be anonymous, went with us on numerous distributions. She and John, her husband, would raise money and were great volunteers. Sometimes Mary would take a girlfriend with her. She would play tennis with Danny Quintana and helped with the sports camps and everything else. John had a great sense of humor and went with us on a couple of trips. They were very successful and reached into their pocket and helped out. This was important. They not only donated money but they took the time to actually help out.

We had a board of directors who stepped in and helped me navigate the tough stuff. Our board consisted of Assistant Pastor Russ Reuther, Michiel Shaw, Buzz Holms and Jim Wilson. They had all been in the field with us and loved the ministry. We were more like a family than co-workers. We all loved what we did. We would always say that the details at home were work but the payday is in the field. This is where we all shined. We would tag some of the wheelchairs we collected from individuals and put their name on them so we could track them.

After the distribution, we would then send the people or the hospital or nursing facility who donated the wheelchair a picture with the person who received it. Some people had lost loved ones and donated their wheelchairs. They found some comfort knowing that someone in need got use from this equipment. It brought a smile to their faces knowing a loved one's wheelchair was still helping someone else.

As we grew, so did the need for wheelchairs. We were like the boy throwing starfish back into the ocean. We could not help everyone but we helped as many as our time and resources allowed. It just saddens us that there was so much more to do.

Chapter Five

The Middle East: We Are Not a Christian Organization

"A man's wisdom gives him patience; it is to his glory to overlook an offense"

Proverbs 19:11 NIV

The Mobility Project was not a "Christian" organization. We were simply a non-profit 501(c)3 that delivered wheelchairs to the poorest people on the planet. We gave disabled people hope and a new lease on life. Our spirituality was just a personal choice for those of us that were involved. This allowed us to go to countries like Afghanistan without all the hassle of explaining our faith. You did not have to be a "Christian" to go with us or to receive a wheelchair as some organizations were religion-based and biased. We worked with anyone who had a heart to serve. We had many people who were spiritual but not religious. Some were even atheists.

In Afghanistan, Pakistan and other Islamic countries, some of our volunteers were Muslim. In Thailand, many were Buddhists. We are Christians and we do not deny our faith. We don't shove it down people's throats. We also believe people can be good people and not share our beliefs. We believe that being a Christian is a way of life. It is a verb, not a noun. The bible explains this: *"In the same way, faith by itself, if it is not accompanied by action, is dead." James 2:17*

It's like Jeff was telling Danny one time when someone told them they were a Christian. He asked, "Oh, what do you do?" — meaning what is your Christian calling. Most of the time people did not get it. Being a Christian is not a label, it is a way of life.

Our volunteers — Christian and non-Christian — were amazing. They paid their own way and rarely complained about the housing arrangements, the food or the conditions. Sometimes it was pretty rough in the field. When you work with the poorest of the poor, you see the whole world in a new light. The difficulties you thought were problems back home were minor events and nothing to get terribly worked up about.

Your First World bubble bursts wide open to a world you never knew existed or believed could exist. You see the true face of poverty and suffering. The picture of lifting a person off the ground and giving them the gift of hope, dignity along with independence is indescribable. They got mobility and we were the ones receiving the best gift of all. Some Christians compared it to the washing of a persons' feet as Jesus did in the Bible. Maybe. But who were we to be compared to Jesus? This always made me very uncomfortable.

Before 9/11, in 2000 we made our first trip to the Middle East. Jeff went ahead of me with Steve Oliver and Ray Terrill. They were going to Pakistan and had to drive over the Khyber Pass to get into Afghanistan. This was a grueling 10-hour-plus ride. I stayed behind to bring the team into Pakistan. We would distribute the rest of the wheelchairs when they returned from Afghanistan.

The airport into Kabul was not open. The runways were blown up. Kabul, Afghanistan's capital city, was occupied by the Taliban. Jeff did not want me to go at this time. It was just too dangerous.

A ministry called Morning Star was already in-country and had several projects. They employed women to make blankets and supported the one "secret" Christian church that existed at that time. They focused on women and children with a language school. They distributed the blankets and food to smaller villages. They financed the shipping of the wheelchairs to the country. This was always the most difficult part of any distribution.

We often partnered with ministries and missionaries in a country who could identify the need. If they could get sponsorship for the shipping we were always on board. This was before the attack on America. The U.S. military was not helping us yet through the Navy's Project Handclasp.

Jeff, Ray and Steve left for Afghanistan. When they crossed the border, they were interrogated by the Taliban. Then they were appointed an armed guard to drive over the pass with them. The guard was not there to protect them but to keep them in line. No books, no pictures, cameras or videos were allowed. The Taliban are far worse than reported in the mass media. They did not allow any music, television, movies and the only publicly approved activity was prayer. These horrible religious terrorists are one of the worst violators of human rights in the history of the world. They must hate women because they treat them like less than property.

There are trees along the road and in Kabul itself where they would confiscate the videos and tear the tape and wrap it around the branches. This was a statement from the Taliban, a warning if you will. There were several checkpoints on the way.

Jeff was asked directly by a border guard if he was a Christian. He said he was. Someone in the group tapped him from behind to tell him to deny that he was a Christian. Jeff would never deny this fact. The guard asked him again "What?" Jeff repeated, "Yes, I am." The guard said, "Usually everyone lies. I suggest that when you get stopped again that you keep that to yourself." Jeff would give his life for the Lord and is fearless. He would never deny his Christian faith regardless of the danger. At the time Jeff was assessing whether or not they would shoot him. Nobody had ever said that. Jeff understood that if you deny the Lord, you might pay for your denial in the afterlife.

The Taliban always assumed every person in the country from the United States was a Christian and they were probably correct. Regardless, during this time there were very few Americans in the country. The non-profits that were there kept to themselves. Big international organizations that were in country never came out of their compound. The only time they were seen was to leave and another group would come in to replace them. But they were able to raise millions and do nothing or virtually nothing.

This always amazed me, as these were people working in high-paying jobs and they literally did nothing. The general public donates more money to non-profits that are basically scams and we always struggled financially. These huge non-profit organizations have massive payrolls. The CEOs often make over $500,000 a year. We were there doing the work as volunteers and paying our own way.

On rare occasions, Jeff was able to call me from Afghanistan. I had never heard him sound like he did on these few phone calls. His voice was a whisper. He did not want anyone to overhear the conversation even though he was in a safe house rented by the Morning Star Ministry. The Taliban were killers who had taken over a country. Jeff was concerned about everyone's safety. He said the darkness was everywhere. Most of the roads were dirt, all the buildings blown up, billions of bullet holes and the local people living in constant fear for their lives. He said he had never seen anything like it. They distributed wheelchairs in a blown-up Russian apartment building. To top it off, they were on the second floor, as the first floor was the toilet. Jeff said that he had to dress like the local men. Disabled people had to go up the stairs to the distribution.

They grew beards before they went in country so they could blend with the locals and not offend the Taliban. It was against the law to shave. The distribution was Taliban-driven. They only had men there to receive the wheelchairs. They were only allowing them to give the wheelchairs to the wounded Taliban soldiers. Jeff saw a young woman being carried to the distribution. Her family put her on the ground. The family must have lived close by. She was covered from head to toe in scarves or a shalwar kameez, a local traditional clothing for Afghan women.

Jeff went over to the lady to help her. The Virtue and Vice Police told him he could not give her a wheelchair, only the men. He waited for them to go to the other side of the building and he quickly got her a wheelchair as the family cried and thanked him. The family hurried and left the building.

The Virtue and Vice Police would make sure everyone's clothing was correct. One day, as Jeff left the compound, he was wearing the kameez pants over his Levi pants. He said he did not like how they felt. They are very lightweight cotton, very baggy and felt like pajamas. Soon we were all quite comfortable in them, what's not to like? The police hit him on his back, grabbed his pant leg and began shaking it, yelling and screaming. He had to go back into the house to change out of his Levis.

Generally, if a woman looked a man in the eye, or if she was not covered completely or walking behind a man or if she was alone, she would be beaten immediately. They enjoyed their job. You could not fight back or assault them or they would kill you. They could hurt your Afghan volunteers after you left. Imagine walking down the street and some jerk hitting you if you were wearing the wrong pants.

The Taliban were the federal killers. The Taliban had AK47s. The Virtue and Vice police were the local religious nut jobs. They had little sticks to hit you and remind you that you needed to abide by their crazy rules. Some of their guards were not the brightest. They would carry grenade launchers and point them at people. They were stupid, mean, evil little creeps. There was no plan for their society. Jeff knew a lot about guns and was not intimidated by them, but he was upset by how these evil bastards treated the public.

Some of the Taliban were recruited from their homes and did not want to be there. When the Americans came in, some of the Taliban just took off their black turbans and went home. Others went over the border to Pakistan. They wanted to do damage to Westerners.

If a husband, brother or father did not keep his wife in line, the Religious Police would step in. She would also be hit with sticks or even arrested. At this time, all women were required to wear a Burqa. The faces must be covered at all times.

The Taliban practice an extremist Wahhabi version of Sunni Islam. When Afghans violated the many draconian religious laws, they got arrested and ended up in Kabul's stadium. The Taliban used the stadium for sadistic public entertainment. They would force people to attend and watch as they covered their victims' heads with bags and executed them after a long drawn out public display of yelling, screaming and beating.

Jeff said the whole city looked like a moonscape. We called it the Wild West. I did not go into Afghanistan until after 9/11 when the Taliban had been run out and our military was in place in the year 2002. The people were so grateful and relieved. I can only imagine that it was like Poland after liberation from the Nazis.

On the way back into Pakistan, Steve, Jeff, Ray and their volunteers stopped for a bathroom break. Steve had left the car and run out into a field of land mines to relieve himself. Jeff said "Hey, you are in a mine field." The rocks were painted red to point this out to the local people. This is where most of the non-war injuries occurred. Steve's eyes were as big as saucers. Jeff told him to put his fingers in his ears and walk back carefully on his exact footprints. Jeff finally stepped over the rock and stepped on a couple of his footprints. This convinced Steve to come back. Steve never made that mistake again. After he made it back, Jeff started laughing. Steve was not amused.

The country is saturated with land mines and 60 people a month lose limbs, many of them children. There are no accurate government statistics on the total number of people with disabilities. Some estimates claim over 20 percent of the country have some type of disability. There is no accurate government data on anything as this country does not have a functioning government. We have not been there since 2004, so we do not know how much progress is made, if any. We do know that if the Taliban takes that country back, it will be a total and complete humanitarian disaster. Financing for the Taliban came from the Saudi Royal Family.

As they were making the grueling drive over the pass at night, Jeff said he was deep in thought as to how this situation could happen anywhere in the world. He felt we as a country were dropping the ball and he was appalled. We researched and read many books to get answers. The best one was "Charlie Wilson's War." There was an excellent movie made about the book, starring Tom Hanks.

Once we could start flying directly into Afghanistan two years later, it was the most shocking experiences I ever had. We had to fly the groups in because it was so difficult and dangerous to travel over land. Ariana Airlines planes were old 727s and super rundown. We would jokingly refer to the airline as "Scariana Airlines." We actually flew in an old Mexicana airplane our first couple of trips. Pretty funny as all signs were in Spanish: "remain seated," "bathroom," etc. We thought this might be why no one followed any rules. The men went to the bathrooms and smoked openly. They sat or stood anywhere and everywhere, aisle or floor, they did not care. They would get up as the plane was landing to get their bags and set them in the aisle. Then the landing was very rough due to the blown-up runway.

I remember our first time landing in 2002. All of our mouths were wide open. The scene was from an apocalypse movie. The air was thick with dust. There were burned-out and blown-up buildings everywhere. There were tons of shrapnel all over the runway and on the sides. There were destroyed tanks and jeeps on one side of the runway. There were planes that were destroyed on the other side.

We walked off the plane, walked into the "airport" and stood in line to get our passports checked for visas, etc. We had to explain why we were there and what we were doing. Then there was a mad dash to find our bags. They came into the building on a makeshift belt and were removed immediately and thrown around the room. This was so confusing as the whole airport was the size of a midsized grocery store, if that. It was so crowded. There were special forces from all over the world and men with guns everywhere.

Armed men and local Afghans were pushing and shoving everyone. They were yelling and hitting each other amid lots of arguing. What I remember most is it was very loud. The one good thing is that men were not allowed to look at women, let alone touch them. Women were treated so poorly. If there was a line of any kind, women were allowed to go straight to the front. They did this because they wanted the women in and out. We were not to be in public for too long. They consider women a distraction. Our volunteers, especially our women, would ask me why their women allowed themselves to be treated this way.

First of all, they did not know any other way. The Afghans looked at it as a sign of respect. The family did not want to "show off" their women. A loved and respected woman wore a burqa in public always. They almost saw it as a sanctuary. You can wear anything underneath your burqa. No makeup was needed. When wearing a burqa you could be whoever you wanted to be. They all looked exactly alike.

I wore a burqa one time to the market. I wanted to see how it felt and it was quite comforting. I was hiding in plain sight, so to speak. Our in-country hosts suggested that we wear it to blend in. If you were light-skinned and had blonde hair, you could get away with just wearing the head covering. I am darker in skin tone and look a bit Afghan. They told me I would appear to be an Afghan refusing to wear a burqa and this would not look good for them or me. We were always aware of our hosts' safety. We would eventually leave the country, but they were stuck there. Being prudent in our behaviors was therefore very important.

We had to change into a shalwar kameez before getting off the plane. Our heads had to be covered. I never covered my face unless I was in a dangerous situation. This sometimes happened.

We were doing the first distribution in a small village. We were appointed the regular "guards" for the whole day. Only the men were allowed to do the seating. We women had to stay outside at a table where we did the administration. They did allow us to take a picture of the people receiving the chairs for the first time. But we were not allowed to take any other pictures of the area or any candid shots. We had to put up a fight to be able to do any administration at all.

We explained that if we could not keep track and document who was receiving the chairs, we would not be able to return. Everywhere we went all over the world, we carefully documented who got a wheelchair. We did this for many reasons. One of them was to be certain the people that got wheelchairs needed them. And we always wanted to be credible with our fund raisers. If they could see what was going to whom, it made fund-raising better.

Our volunteers were in a building fitting the men in wheelchairs. We noticed the women and children sitting around the corner under some trees. I asked Steve to find out if they needed chairs and he did. They told him "only if there were any left after all the men were taken care of. I had learned from my time in the Middle East that only educated women were allowed to enter a building and remove the scarf from their heads.

I did this regularly. I also looked men straight in the eye and made them shake my hand when I was leading distributions. I dealt with people in government, directors of ministries and the very wealthy. I felt I was respected by them and we were doing a great thing for their country when very few people were doing anything at all. With this in mind, when I found out they were making the women and children wait, I marched right over to them and tried to motion them over. We knew we would not have enough wheelchairs for everyone.

The guard came to me and told me "no" and I said "yes" and kept walking. He then put his gun right to my chest. I took my hand and moved it. I went to Wakil, our in-country partner and explained it to him. After a very elevated, loud conversation with hands flying and gestures made, it was set. I was able to take just one woman or one child at a time. They took care of them quickly and took their time with the men. All the women and children received wheelchairs that day.

They also requested a woman do the seating when they saw how "hands-on" it was and Alex was then able to help them in the building. At lunch, they had some fruit and rice brought in and the guard who pointed the gun at me came up to me and offered me a banana. Jeff and Steve looked at each other and said, "What is going on?" I said, "Nothing." Maybe it's because I was not eating. I did not eat a lot of local food due to stomach issues. I think the guard was apologizing. I did not tell Jeff about the gun until months later. He would have said, "This is why you could not go on the first trip to Afghanistan."

I had a procedures manual that all the group members had to know before entering the country. There is a very strict, specific dress code for men and women. We had several outfits we could loan them and once they got in-country they would purchase some things. All my outfits were purchased in Pakistan as we made several trips there in 2000-2002. Some women would make their own outfits. I also had some made by a very dear friend from church.

With substantial help from the West, life for Afghans did slightly improve. It was so wonderful to watch the country grow and become safer. We went there so often we rented a guest house and had some employees to run it. By 2003, more and more ministries were looking to serve in Afghanistan. We were hoping to generate enough money to pay the monthly rent and the employees. They were rebuilding rapidly, trying to repair the country one house at a time.

We were able to get on the military base and six solders actually came on the distribution with us. They were with us every day including the sports camp in the stadium. They all told us that this was the most rewarding thing they had done to date in the country. Many of them were helping with the seating, measuring people and picking out the wheelchairs. Playing with the children and comforting the parents, lifting them off the ground was always the greatest impact of all.

Bringing people in wheelchairs with us to help give wheelchairs away was a very important part of the ministry. These people were so embarrassed that they were disabled, it helped them to see volunteers and staff with a disability. They could see well-adjusted, well-educated individuals living and loving their lives. This gave them hope. We did not just put them in chairs. We spoke to them through translators. We asked them about their lives and tried to fit the adjusting of the wheelchair to their everyday life. For example, if the individual was working in an office and had total use of their hands, we would offer a light, easy-to-maneuver wheelchair.

Some men just wanted a PET, (personal energy transport) as they were called. These were hand-driven carts they could use to transport themselves to work. Some people could walk despite their injuries and we would supply walkers and crutches. We had some toilet chairs that were a huge blessing. All the toilets were a hole in the ground. This is typical of the Middle East. Once they were given a wheelchair, they could then transfer directly to a commode rather than having to climb down to the ground, get really dirty, use a hole in the ground as a toilet and try to climb back up to the wheelchair.

The wheelchairs also helped parents by not having to carry their loved ones. This made them more independent. Children sometimes have the greatest needs of all. The most important thing was to make the chair useful for whatever school situation they were looking at, if their children were able to go to school.

Afghanistan was the only country where we brought every piece and type of equipment we could find. In every other country, there were items left over that we would donate to a facility or hospital. In Afghanistan, every item was used — even the cardboard boxes for packaging. We used old gallon water bottles for packing and the people also wanted these items. They made use of everything. It was truly amazing. After our long distribution days with the military helping us, we were blessed with a great American meal, shared with the troops at the base. We could also purchase Cheerios at the PX, which made our day.

Downtown Kabul was like a scene out of the 1800s. There were more horses, camels and donkeys than cars. The shops were barebones. Bikes were also used to deliver "naan" (the local bread). They tied naan on the back of the bike. There were no shopping bags. Right down the street from our house was a butcher shop of sorts built under a tarp held up with sticks on all four sides. They would butcher the goats right there in front of you. Not many butcher shops had the luxury of a refrigerator.

I remember bringing volunteers in and riding by these butcher shops. They would be horrified, blood was everywhere and no reaction from the locals at all. Small children and families would walk by like the butcher shops were not even there. One of the volunteers turned to me and said, "At least we were not going to get our meat there." I laughed, "yeah, right." I don't know where they thought we would get it? I gave it to her straight and asked her if she wanted to be a vegetarian on this trip and she said, "Maybe".

The smell of the Third World is similar everywhere we have been. Mostly it's the burning of fields, trash and the smell of cooking out in the open with amazing spices. Downtown, in order to make money, young men would carry around cans with smoke coming out of them. They would put their faces up against our vehicle, asking if we wanted their services. They were chasing away evil spirits. Locals would pay them for this service.

There was an excellent book, "The Kite Runner," that was made into a movie. The movie was done so well and brought back so many memories, I turned to Jeff and told him I could smell the country. This is the best movie I have ever seen about Afghanistan and one of my favorite books of all time. I could see the dust in the dirt roads and see the desperation of the people. Their haunting looks of war will live with me forever.

Part Two
A World Full of Disabled

Chapter Six

So Many Countries, So Little Time

"And without faith it is impossible to please God, because anyone who comes to him must believe that he exists and that he rewards those who earnestly seek him."

Hebrews 11:6 NIV

Lisa and friend in Vietnam 2001

By the second year of our calling, we were traveling so much that Jeff would be in Russia with Ray and their volunteers. I would be in El Salvador with Steve and our volunteers. Each team was distributing up to 200 wheelchairs. We had so many outreaches going that we had to divide and conquer. The need was and is great. We did not want to turn down anyone that needed a wheelchair.

Jeff had his own business. This enabled us to do our Christian duty and engage in constant travel. We knew going in that Jeff would travel a great deal. It was about this time when we came up with a policy that married couples could not be away from each other more than two weeks.

In October of 2003, Jeff and I went to Afghanistan together and distributed wheelchairs. He went home for about a week. I stayed in Afghanistan with Steve, Miriam and Ray. We had global planning and other business to discuss. We had some wheelchairs brought into Uzbekistan where we were going to work with the local missionaries to distribute them. Jeff flew into Kazakhstan and met us in Uzbekistan. This turned our lives into an incredible humanitarian adventure.

Every time we spoke at an event, there were requests for wheelchairs. Every church had an outreach somewhere in the world. They knew people with disabilities and our Mobility Project could work with them. Consequently, with just word of mouth among churches and other non-profits, we had more people needing wheelchairs than we had the time or resources to deliver them.

Jeff and I were in Vietnam and watching the BBC. There was an extreme weather problem in Mexico. Pakistani politics was a topic and, of course, the search for Osama Bin Laden. All of these news reports were within about three minutes of each other. I looked at Jeff and said, "Wow, I never would have believed if someone told us that one day we would be in Vietnam, three countries were in the news, and we had been to all three." We had been to all of the same cities that were in the news globally that day.

Re-entry to the United States was very difficult. Our experience was common. Generally, when missionaries are out of the country for a year or two at a time they had a program in place to debrief them. Coming home can be extremely difficult to explain to others. People in the comfort of the United States would never understand what we just experienced, not even our own families. They wanted to understand and help but they simply could not comprehend the desperation of the disabled poor unless they joined us in the field. Re-entry to an opulent society can lead to depression even if these distributions were the best experiences of our lives. They did not understand just how poor other people live and how much help we were providing.

Listening to people complain about the price of gas, the weather or other little First World problems was difficult. I remember going to our Bible study in between trips as they were a great support team for us and they were all dear friends. Some of the prayer requests almost sounded selfish. We had to check ourselves constantly. These requests were important to the people who made them. We needed to respect that — and we always did. Jeff and I have each other, God's love and our family. That is what is important.

At ladies' Bible study, what was relevant to me was that my life was very different than that of other women. I was a 42-year-old grandma, for goodness sake. And wheelchair distributions had become my life.

There were wealthy people praying for new swimming pools and some for an early close on their new million-dollar home. Don't get me wrong, some of these women turned into our greatest supporters. One doctor and his wife were amazing. We did not have insurance so he and his wife decided to treat us for free and did so for years. He always made sure our shots were up to date and took care of our many illnesses when we returned. We were very sick a few times. Jets full of people are germ incubators.

I got so sick in Mexico I was not able to fly straight home because I had dysentery. When we were going through customs in Los Angeles, I had to be treated in the hospital before I was able to get back on the plane. Thank God Jeff was with me on this trip.

On another trip from Pakistan, Jeff was so sick his fever was over 102 as we got on the plane. Sometimes it was the food. Other times it was something else. You could make yourself crazy trying to figure out exactly what it was. When we first started these trips, I would bring all my own food. Soon I got complacent and Jeff was just fearless.

Few people are completely healthy. We all have our own medical issues but might not need a wheelchair. The reason I had stomach issues was due to a surgery in 1997. I was rushed to the ER with horrible gut-stabbing pains. I had experienced stomach pain my whole life. This was much worse. I was tested when I was younger and they could never figure out what it was. Finally, they gave me a blanket diagnosis of colitis. I never had colitis.

It was late at night, they gave me morphine, stuck a tube down my throat to release gas and said I would have to wait until the morning for a specialist to arrive. I was screaming and crying it hurt so bad. I asked Jeff to pray with me to have the Lord take me as I knew I could not go on.

He called the emergency room doctor into the room and grabbed him by his shirt, saying, "You had better get a doctor in here right now because my wife is in so much pain she wants to die." Jeff went on to say that I had three children all natural and I could take a lot of pain. He then told him to call the doctor now! If it was his wife, he would have done it immediately. They called the doctor.

After an ultrasound I went into surgery; still, they did not know what it was. When they opened me up, they found my intestines were all twisted up in my stomach. They could have burst and I would have died had they waited much longer. The doctor said my intestines were loose and this must have been a birth defect. When I had pain in the past, it would twist a little and simply untwist itself. This could not be seen on any test. It would not show up unless the intestines were twisted at the time.

To top it off, a couple of days later I had an infection and they had to open me up and drain it and I was to heal with an open wound in bed for six to eight weeks. This is where Jeff first got his experience in wound care. I had home healthcare for a while, but then Jeff had to take over. I was depressed. I wondered why God did not take me and why I was still here. I began to read my Bible and it made sense to me for the first time ever.

I believed in God, but I did not have the faith Jeff had from his traumatic experience in not using drugs. I did not grow up in a family of faith. My dad was an atheist. My maternal grandmother is Jewish. My maternal grandfather was Mormon. This combination resulted in a non-religious upbringing for my mother and me and my sister. Still, I had a great childhood. It was just not spiritual.

Now I had a traumatic situation and for the first time in life everything made sense. I have a huge scar and tell people to this day that is where God entered my body, not knowing he had been there the whole time. A short time later, we were in Nicaragua with the Mobility

Project. God let me live and had an awesome plan for my life. It was going to be amazing.

The travel was brutal, but we had many perks. Our supporters saw the toll it was taking on us both and recognized the re-entry problem. Jeff always said we went to every country nobody ever wanted to visit. However, we went through great countries and cities that we did want to visit. We would stop in Paris, Brussels, Lisbon on our way to the Middle East or Africa. Our supporters suggested we take a couple of days of furlough instead of coming straight home. This would give us time to reflect and me time to write.

The only way to get to Afghanistan was to go through Dubai. This city is beautiful and a very stark contrast to Afghanistan. Dubai is a rich city located in the United Arab Emirates. The UAE is one of the wealthiest countries in the world, sitting right on the Persian Gulf. We were able to go through Germany, where Ryan, our oldest son, was stationed. He was already planning to enlist immediately before the 9/11 terrorist attacks. After 9/11 we asked if he was still going in and he said "Hell yes." Ryan is fearless and tough like Jeff.

One time we were in Mexico City and our in-country hosts had a house in Acapulco. He insisted Jeff and I stay there for a few days. We were so blessed in many ways and the generosity of others always helped us in our service of the Lord.

After the terrorist attack on the United States, things changed dramatically as we all have come to know. We already had a container of wheelchairs on the way to Pakistan. This was one of our first post-9/11 trips. People were terrified for us. We should have been terrified, but we knew we were doing the Lord's work.

We had this sense of calm and peace and were not afraid. Our in-country hosts even said we should put off the trip. We did not. We had a skeleton crew for this one. Bin Laden was believed to be hiding in Pakistan. As we found out later, he was. Having seen the work of the Taliban and Al Qaeda first hand, they are the modern face of evil in the world today.

Chapter Seven

Traveling After 9/11

"Now Faith is being sure of what we Hope for and certain of what we do not see"

Hebrews 11:1 NIV

Blanket and food distribution Afghanistan 2002

After the 9/11 attack, things changed dramatically. Prior to the attack, we had a container of wheelchairs on the way to Pakistan. This was one of our first trips following this terrible disaster.

We thought we were being responsible to our supporters who had provided funds and chairs for the trip. Our group was Ray Terrill, Jeff, myself, and Alex Rice and two church volunteers who remained of those who originally signed up to go. This was one of the smallest groups we had ever had in the field.

Mike, one of the volunteers, was a representative from the church that helped finance the shipping costs of the container. They supported a tiny church in Quetta, Pakistan, right on the Afghanistan border.

Jeff nicknamed him "Chinese Mike". He was a super great guy. He got this nickname because he gave us his description and Jeff had to pick him out of 100s of people at the airport. Again, with no phone service, pictures were not easily sent back then. The times were different. Mike said the best description that would set him apart was that he was a "6-ft. tall Chinese guy". His nickname stuck.

This turned into one of the funniest and scariest incidents with picking a stranger up in a foreign country we ever encountered. This was something we had done dozens of times before without a problem. Jeff went to the airport and could not find him. Jeff noticed an Asian fellow who was waiting. Jeff asked him if his name was Mike. The gentleman responded saying "yea yea Mike " and then continued with "yea chicken paws". Jeff was confused but knew right away this was not our Mike. Our volunteer spoke English.

Suddenly, a van drove up. Chinese Mike got out of the car in front of the airport with a hamburger in hand. Jeff asked, "Hey! are you Mike?" He said "Yes." The other gentlemen Jeff had spoken to, the other Mike, jumped in the car and they were off. Jeff said "What happened, where have you been?"

Mike said he got off the plane, walked out of the airport where several men met him, took his bags and led him to a car and he was off. They were holding a sign that said "Mike". Our volunteer, Chinese Mike thought it a bit strange. They were polite and he thought maybe something had happened and we were not able to pick him up for some reason. Mike said they ended up at a McDonalds. They seemed concerned he might be hungry. This is where he heard the term "chicken paw."

No, no, I don't know what you are talking about. You have the wrong person!" He said then they realized he was the wrong "Mike." The men were so frantic they put him and his hamburger in the car right away and were back to the airport in just minutes.

This had been right after a journalist had been kidnapped in Karachi. Good people in these countries are just as frightened of terrorists as we are. They want nothing to do with them. We were later told these men were just chicken farmers trying to expand their business by selling the chicken "paws" or feet to the Koreans. That is why the "Mike" at the airport said, "chicken paw." Everything turned out fine. We laughed about this for years. This became known as the great "chicken paw" incident."

We had a container that had been over there for several months. Two more containers were scheduled to be shipped in the coming months. Ray simply wanted to get the job done. Faith can move mountains and get you through the most difficult of times. Again, with scripture as our guide, "I can do everything through God who gives me strength" Philippians: 4:13.

Faith for me is knowing we have all been saved by the grace of the Lord for His purpose. This was our calling. There was never a doubt this was our purpose. Some people might ask, "why risk what could be your life to deliver wheelchairs on the other side of the world?" They did not understand our work. It was simple to us. We had all the confidence from our faith in God that He would protect us. When we are doing the Lord's work, there is no fear in our hearts.

We justified to our fearful family and friends that we were going to Pakistan, not Afghanistan. That is where the real danger existed as we were well aware from our previous distributions to that poor war-torn country.

Our contacts and volunteers in Pakistan were a bit calmer than our Afghan contacts. And, we were working with a very politically prominent Pakistani family in-country. We felt safe. Our supporters prayed like never before. We left the U.S. once again on what was to us just another wheelchair distribution. Our supporters, sponsors, our home church, and family members continued to be our lifeline and support system.

When we landed, our hosts' employees immediately picked us up. They took us to the host family's new home. Our in-country hosts were very accommodating but, as always, they gave us strict rules once we arrived. We stayed with them in their large house. We were not allowed to go or do anything without their knowledge.

There were two reasons for these safety restrictions: One, they were Pakistan political "royalty." And two, what we did was a reflection on them. They were well aware of the 9/11 tension. All of us knew we were not perfectly safe. We could not come and go as we pleased. Our faith in God does not mean the forces of evil do not exist or we can just take them lightly. We were not reckless in our faith. We knew what we could and could not do, is all.

We were comfortable and confident with our host family. We had previously partnered with them at least four other times and knew them well. We will call them the Goodmans to protect their identity. Given the hatred that exists and the evil we have in the world, we do not need to put people in harm's way.

Young Mr. Goodman was in his 30s. Jeff and I were in our 40s at this time. We got along well and had many fruitful and fun times together. From the time we first met in early 2000 to 2002, with each distribution, we had more confidence in them and they in us.

When we were with the young Mr. Goodman, it was very different than being at his parents' home gatherings and political events. There we followed the very strict cultural protocol of women in one room and all the men in the other room. Segregation was the expected behavior. Never once did I see the rule broken. No one seemed to care. All women wore head coverings on their way to the home. They were only able to take off the head covering when in a room occupied by women. The senior Mr. and Mrs. Goodman had prepared me for social gatherings in advance. They knew I was not just a secretary but someone who needed to know what was being discussed in the meetings. Behind closed doors, Mrs. Goodman was also very involved in her husband's business. I took note of this behavior as this seemed to be the case all over the world. Publicly, the women appear powerless. Behind closed doors, they had real decision-making ability.

Some questions that were being discussed were the logistics of the container, the timeline, the number of wheelchairs and mobility devices, the disability group size, etc. These were questions only I could answer. Then I needed to be brought in on the "men's" discussion but was not allowed to participate.

Ms. Goodmen would come to me with questions after her husband explained to her what was needed. This cultural difficulty turned into a crazy game of "telephone." He would ask her a question like "How many kids wheelchairs will be in the shipment of chairs?" Then she would ask me "How many kinds of chairs will be shipped"? These are two very different questions. The language barrier was also a big part of this problem with communication. This was something we had learned to work through over time.

Segregation of sexes was the norm for parties and some formal events. Ms. Goodman explained that they were all brought up this way. They prefer to be around their own sex because it is more comfortable. They have more in common, more to talk about.

She said, "Besides, men smoke stinky things. They scream and make hand gestures. They yell about politics and argue about stupid worldly affairs. I do not want to hear about these matters when I am out with friends." If you think about it, at times, that is how we behave here in the U.S. We hang out with people who become friends because we have common interests.

Ms. Goodman and I became good friends. She was not much older than me. As is their custom, she was married young, at age 14 or 15. As I remember it, she had her first son during their first year of marriage.

Young Mr. Goodman respected both of his parents very much and the love was evident.

When I met with the Pakistani government, I was treated with respect. This was especially true when they found out I was the leader of the trip. Their culture and society were changing. I am sure these political situations are much better now.

Over 20 years have passed since our first distribution to the Middle East. During these early visits we stayed in very modest hotels and we were happy to retire back to them and be able to relax and be ourselves.

The young Mr. Goodman went from a swinging young single man to a married man in 2002. He had a young bride his parents had chosen for him, a baby and large home by this final visit. I had several discussions with him about not knowing who he was going to marry and what he thought about it because it was fascinating to me.

Young Mr. Goodman had attended a prominent university in the United States. He was quite aware of our at times crass American ways. We were always respectful of his culture. He was happy to explain with great candor the cultural differences. He said that this is the way it was supposed to be.

His parents' marriage was arranged by their parents and their parents' marriage by their parents and on and on. I said that I could understand if he had not spent time in the U.S., like we would know everything about his culture. A lot of this was still new to us.

He was gracious and had a sense of humor. He laughed. I realized how ignorant I was to question their cultural traditions. When I think back, I am a bit mortified. Like our culture is the "right way" or the "only" way?

His answer was, "My parents know me better than anyone on earth. They know who will suit me the best. They know what my likes and dislikes are. My mom knows what girls I think are pretty and she certainly knows what type of personality will put up with me." He added, "my parents did not know each other at all.

"Sometimes we will know of the other person or know that they are a cousin of a cousin or something. But it does not matter. My parents grew to love each other as we all do. They grew up to know each other better than anyone else and therefore love each other more than anyone else, but God, of course."

He was right. From what I could see, his wife was an absolutely gorgeous woman inside and out. Their child was beautiful. I am sure things are different now with social media. Their cultural tradition of arranged marriages seemed to work just fine for them.

Since he was so aware of American ways he and Jeff would sit for hours and talk. They joked around and they would discuss the differences and similarities in the Bible and the Quran.

When we arrived on that last visit after 9/11, Young Mr. Goodman, "Bob," as we were on first name basis, was not able to pick us up at the airport. He was busy making arrangements for our distribution and accommodations. Before the terrorist attack, the only thing that kept Bob from picking us up from the airport was Kite flying day or the Basant festival. This was a celebration which lasted at least two days. This is a tradition where men fly kites from roof tops with sharpened wire type strings and sometimes sharpened with glass.

The festival is filled with sweet treats and fun-filled entertainment. The kite competition is the main event. The festival had been cancelled off and on for years and has been banned now for the past ten years. Every new year, the locals are hopeful that the government might vote to allow it once again. There were accidental deaths caused by innocent gun shots into the air when "cutting a kite down to victory." Then there are the hundreds of electrocutions, and the severed body parts from the sharpened kite strings lying in the streets and sidewalks.

The sky looks amazing as it is filled with kites. To this day when you look up at the electric wires in Afghanistan or Pakistan you can see tangled kites high above the streets. This festival was also banned in Afghanistan during the Taliban's barbaric rule.

From what I have read, now in Afghanistan this activity is only legal for men and boys. I liked the book "Kite Runner." I had to ask Bob if this whole kite flying thing was as great as the book made it out to be. He replied, "no, much more." Bob said kite flying were some of his best childhood memories. He and his brothers had a blast with this kite flying festival.

Bob was so happy when we arrived that November, he turned to Jeff and asked if he wanted any Vodka. We were surprised. Pakistan as far we knew had been a dry country. Despite this appearance, they brewed beer and had distilleries and exported Vodka. We had always joked about this hypocrisy. We assumed with Bob's connections he was able to obtain this contraband on special occasions.

In fact, knowing this on our first trip, Jeff was very creative. After a long stressful day, once in a while, we would enjoy a beer or a cocktail just like anyone else in the Western world. There was extra stress being in the Middle East.

Most Christians will say they do not drink. But when you get them in a strange country with people they do not know, doing a stressful job for disabled people in great need, almost everyone will say "Heck yea, I will have a beer at the end of the day."

After completing the distribution of wheelchairs in Lahore and the surrounding areas, the Goodman family said we should leave the wheelchairs in Quetta. Perhaps we should distribute them another time.

I knew this would be almost impossible as we had too much on our plate as it was. The cost and time for us to return at a later date was not feasible. The last thing we wanted was to lose the chairs. No one would know what to do with them. They would just rot, be used for carts or anything but what they were intended.

The people designated to have them would continue crawling on the ground, be carried by family members and friends, or the shut-ins would not leave their home at all. We had to distribute them. The thought of this weighed heavily on us after everything we went through to get them there.

Young Mr. Goodman was running for Parliament. He was very concerned for our safety and how he would look if he let us do the distribution and something happened to us. He and his family genuinely cared for our safety.

Ray Terrill insisted on moving forward because Mike's church was supporting the tiny church in Quetta. This is why Mike came on the trip. He was to follow through for his home church and report back.

Ray was always a bit hard-headed. He was the trip leader on this distribution. Jeff and I or Ray could lead the distribution. But to avoid confusion, one of us was in charge. We did our best and honored that. Against our host's better judgment, we went to Quetta.

The pastor and his family were wonderful. They picked us up. divided us by gender and gave us rooms to stay in. Girls with girls and boys with boys. The weird thing was that we felt like we could not leave our rooms once we were in them. Looking back, it was just a few hours till dinner. I am sure our safety was a big consideration. We slept, played games, wrote and downloaded pictures. They served us a wonderful Pakistani meal and got us up bright and early, ready to distribute the wheelchairs.

Like other distributions, the people came and waited. Men with men, women with women and with children. We tried to serve the women first. The in-country missionaries told us no. They were frightened what might happen to them after we left. So we adjusted.

We did a lot of adjusting on this trip. We had gone to a park and told locals we were from Canada. That was our standard line. They did not buy it.

Much to our surprise, Ray decided to go to the newspaper and have them do a big story on us and the wheelchair distribution project. We were grilled in the park by some locals. Then we were surrounded by a group of men for about 15 minutes. The men kept questioning us individually, moving in closer and raising their voices.

They were upset because the U.S. had just bombed Afghanistan. They kept saying we had no right to bomb other countries. This was a big surprise to us. The people in Afghanistan actually had shown that they liked us on previous visits. Here, the people in Pakistan were mad as hell at us.

I think they were concerned that the US would bomb them, as they knew that Bin Laden was reported to be close by. I was slightly nervous and praying internally.

Jeff and Ray were hiking in the mountains nearby. They could see us but could not hear us at first. When they finally saw what was going on, they immediately returned. I was alone with the volunteers and in-country missionaries. I was trying to explain to the men what we were doing. They were not happy with the fact that I was a woman and seemed to be in charge.

Jeff was able to convince them we were there to help them and meant no harm. Jeff could have a welcoming, calming effect with people and we were able to walk away slowly and return to the vehicle. He told them we had tickets to leave on the next plane out, flights were not daily. This was all we could do and it was a huge relief.

After this incident, Jeff and Mike slept on the roof with the family dog for a couple of nights until we could get a plane out. They had a good vantage point and did not want to be surprised by any crowds or mobs as this is what can happen in these circumstances.

We were all very concerned for the pastor and his sweet little family. They treated us with such kindness. I remember the days that followed. The silence was chilling. There was no television, no radio, just the call to prayer five times daily. The guys listened from the rooftops at night to hear anything and everything to be one step ahead just in case.

The few missionaries we spoke with in town, only two of them from the U.S., told us to always be home by dark. Never be alone and follow and respect all the customs of the local people. We followed their guidance. It was astounding how calm we were.

We would pray constantly with our small group, along with the pastor and his family. "*Let your gentleness be evident to all. The Lord is near. Do not be anxious about anything, but in everything, by prayer and petition, with thanksgiving, present your requests to God. And the peace of God, which transcends all understanding, will guard your hearts and your minds in Christ Jesus.*" *Philippians 4:5-7.*

Our youth group had saved some money to send with us to help Pakistani children. We purchased school supplies for a local orphanage/school. This is where we made it appear as though we were from the Middle East. I dressed the part and Jeff had a beard and dressed like the locals. We shopped with the pastor's wife to get exactly what was needed. We passed the books, clipboards and pens out to the children.

With God's help, we were able to complete the wheelchair distributions by ourselves. We insisted that the local ministries not help us for their own safety. We did not want them harmed after we were gone.

The clearest memory I have from this distribution was receiving the stares from a Taliban man with a missing leg, who was waiting. I was doing my job assisting people. It was easy to tell by the headdress and clothing who he was. My job mainly was to make sure the people were taken care of in a timely, orderly fashion, considering their disability, etc.

The first day, my head piece kept falling off because we moved around and bent down a lot. The head coverings are slippery depending on the material. The local missionaries gave me a slap on the hand as we were in Quetta. This was not a large city like Lahore. Not having my head covered was not acceptable.

The Taliban man was trying to get my attention. I was under strict orders, as a woman I was not to engage with the men. I got the pastor to translate.

I assumed that, as usual, he wanted to go before all the others. To my surprise he was missing a limb but was quite fine with his crutch which was a handmade walking stick from the nearby hills.

He asked if I could please help his granddaughter because they came from far away. They did not want to travel back in the night. I was delighted to find Alex Rice right away and we took the little girl back to fit her. Alex was eager to find exactly what she needed. A small, lightweight, easy-to-propel manual wheelchair.

From what we could tell, the child had a form of spina bifida. She had no control of her legs but fair strength in her upper body. She appeared to be about 5 years old. The wheelchair was perfect for her. She was able to propel in the chair immediately. She was so happy, she smiled with all her might.

When Alex was done fitting her, she kept rocking forward to moved faster to get her grandfather's attention. As soon as we rounded the corner, her grandfather said her name and they both smiled ear to ear, followed by tears of joy. This public display of affection was something a Taliban member was never supposed to do. He was grateful for the help.

He took my hand, shook it and looked at me straight in the eyes. With God's love, at that moment we were not enemies. We were just two grandparents, sharing the moment and an understanding of family and love in this complicated world we live in.

As the New Testament says, *"But I tell you: Love your enemies and pray for those who persecute you that you may be sons of your Father in Heaven." Matthew 5:44-45[a]*. This was our final trip to Pakistan. We began our focus on Afghanistan soon after our return.

Before 9/11, we were questioned and detained by countries in the Middle East. After 9/11, we were detained and questioned by our own country, European countries and Central American governments like Mexico.

It was difficult. However, this was our mission. We were not the only people in the world who traveled as part of our work. Many people complained. This included diplomats. Changes had to be made to keep us safe. There was definitely a learning curve.

When I traveled through England I was detained due to the number of visas I had for Afghanistan and Pakistan alone. They insisted the non-profit was a cover.

I had to make sure I changed out of my Middle Eastern clothing when I was in the West. Just as I had to make sure to change into the proper attire when traveling to the Middle East. It was stressful and made me feel like I had something to hide.

We purchased works of art and various goods not available in the U.S. in countries we visited. We used these items to sell at our fund raisers. These items sold like hotcakes and were great fun for everyone. We would make baskets for each country we had visited that year, filling them with small handmade goodies.

Unfortunately, the men at the fundraisers enjoyed the knifes, machetes and other larger manly things. They looked threatening to security when bringing them out of or into another country. At times we had so many items we had to have team members put them in their bags. Then we would not be questioned as to the quantities of items even though we would never break any laws or go over any amounts set by any governments.

This money that we would make would go right back to the disabled poor. This was the difficult message we could not get across to anyone in Customs. It seemed as if they did not want to understand. There was too much corruption in the world and not enough people just trying to do good.

On one of our trips back from the Middle East, we went through Germany so we could visit our son who was stationed there. I remember being so tired and trying so hard not to be defensive while being detained. They took every last thing out of our bags and asked us over and over and over again why did we go to Afghanistan and Pakistan specifically so often.

After we explained, one man actually said that people in those countries can get their own wheelchairs. Bringing them from so far away was ridiculous. At that point I remember Jeff grabbing my hand at that moment as he knows me better than anyone. I was ready for a fight.

Jeff is not a pushover. He is slow to anger in very stressful situations. *"The one who guards his mouth and Tongue keeps himself out of trouble" Proverbs 21:23 Ultrathin Reference Edition*

Jeff smiled at them and began a fundraising speech explaining how everything worked. How the chairs went from the dumpster to poor people in poor countries. He gave them brochures and pointed out pictures explained how these people crawl on the ground. Their newfound mobility lifted them up and gave them hope. These wheelchairs were from what is seemingly trash in America.

He went on to explain that we had not seen our son for almost a year. That is the only reason we were laying over in Germany for a few days. Jeff choked up as he explained this. I won't go so far as to say these guys shed a tear, but they did start putting all our things back in our bags for us. They stamped our passports and wished us safe travels. We have to remain calm when serving the Lord.

When we arrived back in the U.S. it was much worse. This was supposed to be our safe haven. This is where, when we landed on whatever tarmac to whatever port of entry, we were home. We were safe. But that is not how we were treated.

We should have been better prepared. This terrible tragedy happened here, right under our noses in our United States of America. And here we were all this time, before this tragedy, going back and forth to the very countries where these horrible terrorists were training young boys and men to hate.

Sadly, we were very aware of this hate training. We had previously been in a boys' orphanage in Lahore, Pakistan. They spoke of Osama Bin Ladin and cheered when they heard his name.

We were there with Bob, (our young Pakistani host), working and researching the need in the area. The orphanage had about 100 boys ages 10-16. The people who ran it said it was all they could do to get them to stay and keep them off the streets.

The orphanage's only hope was to give them an education, but most of them stayed for the food and shelter only. The orphanage appeared more like a holding tank for the boys waiting to come of age and be released to the many terrorist training camps in the area.

We did not return as there were no disabled housed in the facility. I have to say I was very relieved. This place really frightened me like no other. I was filled with a scared, terrifying sadness that was difficult to shake. All we could do was pray and we did. These children were being taught to hate everything about the West.

Our port of entry into the United states was Seattle, our home state. They took one look at our passports, took us into the Customs office and there we waited. We were relieved that we did not have to make a connecting flight. However, we waited and waited.

They took us into separate rooms and we began our stories. This took a while. They had to confer with each other to be certain our stories were the same. I remember them being stuck as to why we had a layover in Germany. Why Dubai? Why Turkey, etc.

Our own government detained us. They took a very long time and we were tired from traveling. If you have been traveling for days, you understand. Finally, they let us go.

The agent stamped our passports, as they had many times before and they said "welcome home". I almost dropped to my knees and wanted to cry. This is something we heard every time we came back into the country but this time it was different. This time it meant something. This is my country and they want me here. This is something we should not take for granted and should hold as sacred in our hearts.

Traveling is a gift and an education that you cannot receive by staying put where you live. Had I not had these experiences, I would not have the appreciation for the freedom and security that is our great country.

It was not a job, it was a blessing. Lessons are learned by experience and hard work. I believe God gave us something much more than money, a shiny new car, a large home or things. These things did not come easy to us in these 14 years while in God's service to the disabled poor.

Our travels to the poorest parts of the world and the blessing we had in delivering wheelchairs to God's disabled children gave us the gift of love. We do not care about fancy things. We received the ultimate gift. No one can ever take away our relationship with God. We got to see firsthand His work like never before. We got to serve the Lord.

Sometimes it was like being in a dream. "Who does this?" I would ask myself. Living month to month finding out about needs all over the world and countries we never wanted to visit.

We followed the need, not our desires. We were invited to places some people only read about. It felt surreal most of the time. God gave us the ability to pray through difficulties. We would get a response from God as we worked day to day, not knowing for certain what was ahead. We were open to anything and everything, knowing He was and still is in charge. To sacrifice daily to serve Him is difficult with all the distractions in life. It is well worth it.

There were sacrifices within our family, like being away for birthdays, holidays and missing the small celebrations of everyday life. Thankfully our children understood and never made us feel guilty. They had experienced this blessing of helping others with us. Not all our family members were understanding. We are at peace with the Lord. I hope in my heart one day all of my family members will understand.

Only when we are stripped down and raw can we be real with ourselves and God. To know why I was put here and to be able to actually do it is unexplainable. I pray daily and thank Him to this day for the life He gave us, difficulties and all. When we find our purpose in life and serve the Lord, we have an inner peace that no amount of money can buy. To find your purpose, pray and the Lord will answer your prayers.

Chapter Eight

Kabul

"But when you give a banquet, invite the poor, the crippled, the lame, the blind, and you will be blessed. Although they cannot repay you, you will be repaid at the resurrection of the righteous."

Luke 14:13-14 NIV

Kabul Stadium Afghanistan

Unlike Lisa and Jeff Murphy, I started helping with wheelchair distributions much later into this adventure in humanitarian work. But like all of the people all over the world doing humanitarian work, it has been a wonderful life adventure. I would not trade it for anything.

When I told my family and friends I was going to Afghanistan to help deliver wheelchairs, they were certain I had finally gone over the deep end. If we don't add excitement to our lives, we stagnate. Having traveled to Costa Rica and Mexico with Lisa, Jeff, Richard St. Denis and the many Mobility Project volunteers, I knew the trip would be reasonably safe. By the time I got involved, this organization had already distributed thousands of wheelchairs in over 20 countries.

In Afghanistan, thanks to the U.S. military and our allies, the city was secure enough to safely deliver approximately 1,000 wheelchairs to the poorest of Afghanistan's poor. There are many countries that want wheelchairs. Sometimes it is so dangerous we cannot risk the safety of our volunteers. Thanks to the U.S. military, we were going to be safe.

Our volunteers flew from their various states to New York. From there we flew to the proud capital of the former French Empire, Paris, the city of love. Back in 2004, I could walk on my crutches and braces to the bathroom on the plane. It did not stop my insane back pain from being in an uncomfortable seat for eight hours of flight across the Atlantic. But international travel was doable.

We stayed overnight in Paris to recharge our batteries, then we flew to Dubai. The stopover was short and soon we were on Ariana Airlines on the way to the ancient city of Kabul. As Lisa recalls, the locals call it "Scariana Airlines."

The Afghans used old 727s to fly into Kabul twice daily. At that time, the airport had one runway. On one side, there was a plane that was shot down in one of the numerous firefights that have plagued this war-torn city over the last 40 years. On the other side of the runway were blown up military vehicles as a reminder that war was not a distant memory. The main terminal was peppered with bullet holes and large murals of President Karzai and their national hero, General Ahmad Shah Massoud, the charismatic leader of the Northern Alliance, who was assassinated by Al Qaeda on September 9, 2001.

Once on the ground, ISAF forces kept a visible presence. French, Italian, Spanish, German, Canadian, Belgium and other NATO troops patrolled the streets in heavily armored vehicles armed with 50-caliber machine guns. The locals hardly paid attention to the troops as they rode their bicycles, cabs, horse-drawn carts or walked.

Shops popped up like mushrooms after a rain among the bombed-out buildings. Literally every building that could have been bombed was.

In 2004, a trip to Kabul was like a visit to Berlin after 1945 and the Allied victory.

To understand the level of destruction and suffering of the people, imagine that what happened to the 26 million Afghans occurred on the same scale in America. We would have approximately 16.5 million war dead, 30 million wounded, 30 million refugees, 10 million war widows raising their children alone with limited access to work. There would not be running water unless you lived in a rich neighborhood and had your own well and septic tank. Electricity would be available from 6:00 in the evening until just past midnight. Every building would have bullet holes or only the walls still standing. And there would be 100 million land mines planted in farm fields, paths and playgrounds of America.

Like Poland after the country was liberated from the Nazis, the Afghan people were ecstatic to be finally rid of the Taliban. The Western media did not fully capture the horror and brutality of this extremist religious group, funded by Saudi money and the opium drug trade. They terrorized this wonderful country.

The Taliban had killing quotas. Women were considered just barely above property under their despotic rule. If a woman was in public alone, that was grounds for a severe beating or worse, a public execution. Women were not allowed to work, or have any type of education. The public was not allowed any type of entertainment activity. Television, movies, videos, soccer and kite flying were forbidden. Music was outlawed. The only approved public activity was prayer.

One public event used by the Taliban to keep their brutal control over the people was the use of the soccer stadium to execute people. Approximately once a week, the stadium would be filled with various individuals who had protested the Taliban rule. Some were there because they just simply did not meet with the approval of the extremist Wahhabi religious government.

They were hanged from the goal posts. Others were shot in the center of the soccer field. Some were just maimed, their arms or legs amputated. Meanwhile, the crowds watched, some cheering, others — especially those who were related to the victims — crying. The executions and public amputations left a lasting mark on the people of Kabul. If you kill one, you scare ten thousand.

I was one of three coaches who had the honor to teach some disabled athletes wheelchair sports. In a country where we estimate that 17 percent of the population have a disability, there are plenty of potential disabled athletes. These estimates vary on the number of wheelchairs needed. Some estimates are as high as 2.5 million, others as low as 500,000. We don't know for certain.

The amputees are everywhere. With millions of land mines, at least 60 people per month lose limbs. The Bush administration at that time refused to sign the Land Mines Treaty. This important treaty bans the use of land mines in war and is a positive step in human progress.

Some amputees crawled on the streets begging. Others drove the simple handmade carts we delivered to them to get around. The single-leg amputees just walked with their crutches and tried to get on with their meager lives. Since antibiotics were almost non-existent, the paraplegics died with the first bladder infection or pressure sore. The city's only hospital lacked medicine, enough doctors or even functioning elevators. When I was there in 2004, the hospital did not have running water.

At the distribution, a young Afghan lady came to us with her beautiful blond-haired baby. She asked us to take her baby, who had to be less than a year old, back with us to the United States. Wish that life could be so simple. Any young couple would have loved to adopt that innocent child. The lady had tears in her eyes. We politely declined her offer.

You could spot the former Taliban. They had this look of hatred and evil in their eyes that I will never forget. Some wore traditional black turbans and had long beards. The non-Taliban Afghans were usually clean-shaven. Most of the Taliban were Pashtu. They and their Al Qaeda allies were recognized by only two governments, Saudi Arabia and Pakistan. This extremist government could not have survived without the financial help from the rich Saudi Royal Family and their gulf allies. Our guide Mahboob had numerous members of his immediate family murdered by this evil regime.

I was talking with him once about the war and the overthrow of that evil government. He told me a story of how once he was so discouraged he was walking alone down an empty street of Kabul. He had tears in his eyes and a Taliban soldier came up to him and asked him what he was doing and told him to stop or he would kill him. Mahboob looked at him and told him, crying, "go ahead. Kill me. You already killed all of my family. Look at what you have done to our country."

The Taliban soldier must have remembered a time when that evil government was not in power and life was better. He told Mahboob to keep going and he let him live. The country was completely destroyed by the war. Nothing was gained by years of constant violence.

After our wheelchair distribution at what pretended to be their hospital, the Mobility Project held a three-day sports camp at the soccer stadium. We had approximately 24 amputees and paraplegics. We even had female athletes or at least participants. We insisted that the females be allowed to play sports. Some of the locals objected as it violated their conservative culture. Each evening the horn would blast with the call for prayer. The entire city would come to a complete halt and everyone would participate in evening prayers.

We brought donated sports chairs from the United States. Then we contributed these specialized sports wheelchairs to the Afghan Paralympics Sports Program.

Danny teaching tennis at Kabul's stadium.

Since there are no tennis courts in all of Afghanistan, we made a makeshift tennis court using a volleyball net. The basketball courts were functional. So we put the Afghan athletes in sports wheelchairs and I got to do what I love, play tennis.

Their athletes were just going through the motions. I asked my translator to tell them, "why don't you put your purses down and quit hitting like your grandmothers? Did you shoot at the Russians that way?" The translator said, "no, Mr. Danny, I cannot say that." I told him, "Tell them that." The athletes took up the challenge, "OK boo," which must have meant "bring it on." The harder I pushed them, the more they liked it.

The head of the Afghan Paralympics was a real jerk. He was privileged. He had two pictures of himself on his windshield and was a single-leg amputee. Another single-leg amputee pushed him in his wheelchair. He was always carrying two cell phones and would crowd in front of all of the athletes because he was "special." I nicknamed him "King Cripple."

At the end of the sports camp, we had an argument with him about the sports chairs. We wanted to give them to the athletes and he wanted them for his organization. I looked at one of the athletes and asked, "Is he going to steal the wheelchairs after we are gone?"

Several of the athletes understood English and one looked at me and nodded yes. I called my athletes together. I looked at King Cripple and pointed my finger at him. "Are you going to steal these wheelchairs when we leave?"

"Oh no, Mr. Danny, I would never do that."

I pointed my finger at him. "Well that's good. Because if I find out you stole these wheelchairs, I am going to fly back here and I am going to beat your ass." Everyone started laughing. We must always remember, *"God opposes the proud but gives grace to the humble." James 4:6b*

One of their coaches took me on a private tour of the stadium. He was showing me where people were hanged, shot, beaten. He explained how the Taliban did not give people the opportunity to be heard.

We were at all times protected by some American army personnel. I was talking with one soldier about his job protecting the population. He had short brown hair cut close to his head and was about age 25. He was very well-educated. He was there to protect us. And he did.

As he explained it, he watches every single move everyone makes. When someone walks into a room, he looks at what they are carrying, their body language, age and what is their business there. If he tells them to put their weapon down, this is exactly what he means. The young man was becoming fluent in Dari and worked to understand Afghan culture.

I was impressed with the professionalism of this young soldier. Finally, he told me that if he tells someone to put down their weapon and instead they are going to fire on him or his men, he would kill them when he had to. He knew exactly what he was doing.

Some of the American troops joined in the sports and played with the disabled athletes. They would help us set up and take the equipment back at the end of the day. Without our military, we could not have delivered the wheelchairs or held the sports camp.

The Afghans are extremely competitive. One Afghan athlete was an amputee version of superman. Both his legs had been blown off. He was missing several fingers on his right hand and only had one eye. His goal was to win the Paralympic gold in track and field. He was strong and super-fast. He could speak enough English that I could understand him.

Once their country recovers, their wheelchair athletes will be as fierce in sports competition as they are as warriors. We had a blast. The athletes, coaches and volunteers laughed, played and competed. At the end of the sports camp, we gave them wheelchairs. They gave us flowers and we both went back to our homes with the impression that peace can work.

My hope is that this country recovers. The Afghan people, despite their internal differences, are creative, hard working and determined to revive their nation. Construction was going on everywhere. In most parts of the city, the construction was taking place with tools that were used in the 6th century. The Afghan people were taking mud and straw and making bricks. The city was very crowded with the thousands of refugees who were returning to try to reclaim homes and shops that once flourished.

On my second to last day, some terrorists kidnapped three United Nations workers within blocks of where we were staying. We could see the helicopters combing the streets from the skies in search of the bad guys, but to no avail. The city is one of contradictions. Next to beggars are 10,000- and 15,000-square-foot homes rivaling the beauty of anything in Naples, Florida, or Irvine, California. These homes were alleged to belong to government ministers. Surprisingly, they can manage their $60 per month pay, yet afford such luxury. The lucrative international opium trade has a firm hold on Afghanistan.

On our last day in Afghanistan, we had dinner with the American troops at the military base. Our troops are tough, alert and professional.

Colonel Ramirez and Major John were gracious hosts. They fed us steak and lobster and told us some interesting war stories.

We went shopping at a local market. There were very interesting items which were stamped, "made in Pakistan," which immediately caught my interest. I bought numerous items that I would never be able to buy anywhere in Europe or the States. I purchased a large suitcase so I could carry back all of these items.

The freedom enjoyed by the disabled athletes and people in Kabul would not be possible without our presence. The overthrow of the Taliban and their Al Qaeda allies is not only in the best interest of Afghanistan, but Americans who love freedom and liberty. We need to be thankful for living in a society that has so much and remember those who only have their freedom and dignity.

This wheelchair distribution to Afghanistan made me appreciate the numerous blessings we take for granted here at home, like a hot shower, telephones, the internet and rule of law. In this new century, in a world full of war, hatred, and the millions of disabled, it was true poetic justice to help do something good in a soccer stadium where the Taliban had committed so much evil.

I will always wonder what my fellow athletes in Afghanistan are doing. I seriously doubt they are still alive, with so little work opportunities and no money. How are they getting around without accessible sidewalks, ramps, disabled parking and accessible bathrooms? One pressure sore and they are dead. Hopefully, one day, Afghan athletes will be able to participate in international competition. All of this will be possible if they have peace. With peace come the benefits of liberty and freedom.

Until Wahhabi schools of hatred quit funding these religious terrorists of Al Qaeda, the Taliban, ISIS, and numerous other killers, the world will never have peace. You cannot have peace when children are taught hatred.

Chapter Nine

Costa Rica, the Most Beautiful Country on Earth

"It is beautiful in its loftiness, the joy of the whole Earth."
Psalm 48:2^a NIV

History is important. Central America can best be understood by looking at its long history. Prior to my Spanish ancestors ruling the Western World, the various Native American empires left their imprint on the indigenous populations.

The vast global Spanish Empire collapsed in 1808 after Napoleon invaded Spain. Napoleon installed his brother Joseph Bonaparte as the new emperor over the Americas. The Spanish world refused to be ruled by a French sovereign. The long-term consequences are still being felt today.

The Americans declared their independence from the powerful British Empire. The American Revolution created a global quest for freedom. Soon the French Revolution followed America's example. The overthrow of the European monarchies meant that millions of those who were ruled wanted self-rule.

The American and French revolutions were the two most important political events since the collapse of the Roman Empire. These revolutions changed the entire course of human history. The idea of the divine right of kings ended with French guillotines.

The Americans reached back to ancient Rome and Greece as the republic model for government. These revolutionary ideas of freedom of thought and liberty of expression influenced the entire Western world and to a large degree changed modern civilization. The Spanish world was part of this change.

Spain controlled an empire where the sun never set. From the rising of the sun in the Pyrenees to the sands of the beaches of the Philippines, from present-day Oregon to Argentina, Spain was the modern world's first superpower. When it fell apart, instead of one super state where rich provinces could provide support and lift up the poor colonies of this vast global empire, there evolved 22 poor countries. Most of the Spanish world never recovered from the collapse of the world's largest empire. Costa Rica is part of what was once New Spain. Despite its poverty, Costa Rica is in far better economic condition than its small neighbors.

Costa Rica is breathtaking in its immense beauty. Their country does not have an army and has a rich history of peaceful democratic rule. Their legal system works most of the time and they have the rule of law. Consequently, they enjoy one of the highest standards of living of any Central American country. It is poor but successful.

They depend on ecotourism to survive. Their ecotourism industry is probably the best on the planet. From the beautiful sandy beaches, manicured coffee plantations, to rivers that cut through well-maintained jungles, this place is tourist heaven. But they have their disabled poor who need wheelchairs.

We did two large wheelchair distributions in 2005 and 2006. The flight into San Jose was uneventful. Tourists from all over the Western world fly to this well-preserved environmental heaven.

The Catholics put us up at one of their monasteries on the outskirts of the city. A plump middle-aged Costa Rican cook and her husband fed us. Young maids cleaned our nice rooms in our comfortable surroundings. Birds of various sizes and colors were in the trees and bushes that surrounded this secure compound. A guard was at the entrance and a security fence surrounded the Catholic monastery. Despite being a successful country, Costa Rica had to deal with poverty and dysfunction from their neighbors.

One of the workers was a young, slim Cuban man who escaped that repressive, corrupt, "socialist" government. He worked in Costa Rica while he was trying to figure out a way to get his wife out of that socialist prison. He needed $30 more to buy her a ticket to fly to Costa Rica. I gave him the $30. He was so grateful he was in tears. He could work on reuniting with his soulmate.

Several rich Costa Rican families assisted with this distribution. The international transport company, DHL, delivered the chairs to a wealthy patron's warehouse. The Costa Ricans were very well-organized. The families were gathered in a patio and waiting for a wheelchair for their loved ones.

Focus on the Family, a Christian organization, helped us put together this distribution. Adelita, our Costa Rican volunteer, was instrumental in making this distribution happen. She did a wonderful job and was very pleasant to be around. She was charming.

Just because people are poor does not mean they do not have pride. The recipients were well-dressed, clean and patient. Their disabled loved ones were carried there and seated next to the family members who brought them to the distribution. The families were all seated before a stage where the recipients were waiting their turn for their family member to be fitted in a wheelchair.

The DHL driver was a big man who could drive that semi like nobody's business. He fit that truck into the tiniest of spaces and unloaded it. He would smile and laugh and clearly enjoyed helping his disabled countrymen. The wheelchairs for the distribution were contributed leftovers refurbished in the United States.

Inmates at a prison in Iowa and in other institutions cleaned and repaired the wheelchairs. They prepared them to be reused by someone in need of mobility. The inmates also made special chairs for people who suffered from cerebral palsy. These specialized chairs enabled the CP-disabled to sit comfortably. The inmates like the work because they were doing something nice. They were providing some freedom for prisoners of disability.

People who are afflicted with CP have bodies that do not work because the wiring in the brain does not fire off properly. It does not impair their intelligence. In time, there will probably be a technological solution that will give people with CP greater movement. The nerve centers might be re-wired. For now, they need specialized wheelchairs.

Hope Haven International, a Christian organization, contributed the wheelchairs for a small cost. Hope Haven is based out of Iowa and South Dakota. Hope Haven was one of the main sources of wheelchairs for the Mobility Project. We always knew we could count on them — and we did.

Hope Haven has helped more than 120,000 disabled people get much-needed wheelchairs all over the world. The inmates like doing the work as it gives them a sense of purpose. Everyone wins with their work.

The Costa Rica Rotary Club members volunteered with the distribution. Successful in their poor country, these businessmen and women were generous with their money and time. They understood the purpose of wealth. These successful businessmen and women were among the most responsible people I met anywhere in the world. They fully understood the purpose of financial success.

Like all of our Mobility Project distributions all over the world that Lisa and Jeff Murphy organized, it was very successful. Lisa and Jeff are Christians but not judgmental. Their actions, not their title, is what motivates them to serve the Lord.

Sometimes you just have to listen, learn and take a new direction. Their lives were changed forever. The Creator is always listening to us and answering our prayers. But we have to be willing to listen to the answer. Can you hear the message of love when it reaches out to you? If we are willing to listen to the Lord, our life will change. Be careful what we pray for, because sometimes we get it. Our prayers are answered and the answers are not what we expect. We get what we need, not what we want.

Jeff is fearless and physically strong. Lisa is smart and tough. They were ideally suited for humanitarian work. They could spot a hustle in an instant and were never afraid to make difficult decisions even if others were going to be angered. If a distribution did not pass the smell test and due diligence, they would cancel regardless of how mad people were going to be at their decision.

We were at a large chemical warehouse owned by one of our wealthy partners who helped organize this humanitarian project. This business owner made available his premises. This distribution had lots of children who suffered from cerebral palsy, more than I had ever seen before in one place. Some of these children had been carried by their parents their entire lives. Their twisted bodies made it hard to communicate. Their mothers and fathers could communicate with them, having raised their children since birth. I had a hard time understanding what they were trying to say.

To properly fit someone in a wheelchair is like measuring someone for shoes or a bike. It can't be too large or the recipient will not be able to properly push themselves in their chair. We have to be certain the person has arms that work. It can't be too small or the person won't fit. You measure the width of your rider. Then measure their legs from the back of their buttock to under their knee. Measure their legs from under the knee to the bottom of their feet. Look at what their particular disability is and figure out their needs. See where they are injured. A high-level injury is different from waist-level or partial paralysis. How much do they weigh?

Using this personal health information, we get them the right wheelchair. We set up three work stations with tables. Each team has a leader. One is good with tools. He or she will change out the parts of the wheelchair and adjust it to make it fit exactly right. The back might need an adjustment. The foot rests might need to be raised or lowered. The arm rests might need to be removed. Finally, the rider needs to have a proper cushion.

After they get their wheelchair, it's off to administration to log in their data. We take a picture of the recipient in the chair. Their name and the number of this recipient is on a chalkboard. Then we take a team picture with their family. The Christians ask them if they can pray for them and they gather around the recipient, hold hands and thank the Lord. Then it is on to the next person and the next and the next until we run out of wheelchairs. We have never run out of disabled people.

I was going through the routine and helping Jeff, my team leader. Next to us on the other table was Jim Wilson and his wife Carol. Jim is probably as handy a person as you will find to assist in adjusting wheelchairs or anything mechanical. He had his crew and an interpreter. I was the Spanish interpreter and assistant for our team. Richard and his crew were on the third table.

Some of the Costa Ricans were disabled because of car accidents. Others lost their mobility because of falls at work. One handsome young man was hit while on his way home from work. He had a brain injury in addition to his broken spinal cord. He was patient and understood he would be helped out in the last days of his now shortened life. A wheelchair would vastly improve his quality of life. It would never heal his broken spine or repair his damaged mental function. But his cross would be lighter.

Sometimes you just have to enjoy the moment. One memory that will always bring a smile; we were doing a distribution in a church courtyard. We were seating disabled person after disabled person — some from cerebral palsy, others from accidents, each one with their own story. We were in the front of this grey Catholic church. The Catholic church is a common site throughout Latin America.

One skinny teenage male was really struggling. He was resisting every attempt to seat him in a wheelchair. He kept hitting his head with his right hand and voicing out DADD, DADD, DADD. I guess he was trying to tell us something!

Since he could not talk, he finally struggled free and took off at a dead run. Steve Oliver, then president of the Mobility Project, looked at me, "I don't think so." The young man was autistic. He clearly did not have a walking disability. I put my tools down and hurried as I pushed into a nearby alley. I burst out laughing. I was laughing so hard the local children were looking at me, wondering if I had mental problems.

I did not want to laugh in front of our volunteers. I did not want them to feel insulted for making such an egregious mistake. He did not need a wheelchair. I laughed until tears came to my eyes. I don't think I ever laughed so hard in my entire life. I kept telling myself, "This is too good. Unbelievable, that kid could run like the wind and we were trying to confine him to a wheelchair."

All you get in life are moments in time. I did not bring it up at dinner. Sometimes it's best to leave well enough alone. Correct it and move on.

Our distribution at a chemical warehouse owned by a wealthy Costa Rican family changed my life forever. Prior to that date I would wander aimlessly chasing money and adventure. From that point forward, my life got a new meaning and purpose.

We have to open our heart to the Lord and appreciate our calling to make the world a better place. Only then is our path going to be with a clear purpose and meaning. If we allow the Lord, the Creator of the Universe to guide us to do the right thing, we will be given the answer on what to do to make life better. And no, it is not to be a suicide bomber or to blow up restaurants or shoot young girls in the face who want an education. The Lord will never instruct us to do something evil.

We continued working with family after family, more young people with cerebral palsy, more car and work accidents, more disabled. A cute young Costa Rican couple was well-dressed and carried their daughter. They have been carrying her for all five years she has been alive. We placed their pretty little girl in a wheelchair that was just right for her needs. CP individuals require a different wheelchair than the hard frame chairs my friends use in the United States. Some need an adjustable back and straps to hold them in properly.

The girl's parents were gracious and grateful. "Gracias, gracias a Dios y a usteds por su ayudo." I still had not caught on that this was a huge change in their lives. I was doing the work but was going through the motions. I did not yet understand just how big an impact one little wheelchair carrying one child would have on each family.

When you provide a wheelchair to a disabled individual, their family receives a huge benefit. It is much easier to push a loved one in a wheelchair than it is to carry them on your back or in your arms. This frees up time for the parents and relatives as well as the disabled individual.

The young, clean-cut couple was overcome with joy that their daughter had a wheelchair. It made me smile and I thought to myself, "Ah, no big deal." But it was a big deal. To this family it was a life-changing event.

On our journey toward the end of time, we have a select few "ah ha" moments where we suddenly get it. A lady in her late 30s with bright red hair and green eyes had been carrying her daughter for six years. We placed her cute daughter in a wheelchair that fit her perfectly. The mother started crying. "Gracias, gracias a Dios. Gracias por todo y que Dios te bendiga."

She was crying so much that I looked at her and a tear came to my eye. It finally hit me. This IS really important. It IS a big deal. This is what I need to do the rest of my natural life. The Lord touched my heart. I found my path and purpose in life. The disabled poor in other parts of the world need wheelchairs and I get to help provide them. This means I will get to travel all over the world and help others to gain mobility. After the distribution, we get to explore, shop and make new friends. How cool is that?

"Commit your way to the Lord; trust in Him, and he will act, making your righteousness shine like the dawn" Psalm 37:5-6[a] URE

My recollection is that we gave out more than 500 wheelchairs at this distribution. We had volunteers from various parts of the United States. A church group was there from South Carolina. One couple was from Washington. Others were from California, Arizona, Colorado, Wisconsin and various other states. Two young college students were there from Columbia. The Rotary Club from Costa Rica was immensely helpful.

At night we would drink alcohol and talk about politics and religion. My friend Brock Moller and a couple of other Mobility Project volunteers were having a big discussion about whether or not Jesus is in fact the son of God. I told them that I came to the conclusion that Jesus is the son of God through my study of science and history. When I read the Bible, I came to the opposite conclusion.

Brock argued that it is impossible to conclude Jesus is the son of God from studying science and history. Only through the Bible can you understand the word of God. Beer does not make you smarter. It only makes you argue more. Fortunately, I was drinking wine. My understanding is Jesus drank red wine.

Every other year I don't drink. This was my drinking year. Is Jesus the son of "GOD"? Yes, I know He is. With others, it depends on what you believe. My Muslim friends believe Jesus was the last great prophet. Jesus is mentioned more times in the Quran than Mohammed. My Mormon friends believe Jesus preached in North and South America and Indians are a lost tribe of Israel. From their portrayals of him, Jesus was Norwegian with light brown hair, white skin and blue eyes.

My Buddhist and Hindu friends really don't express strong opinions about Jesus being "the son of God." My atheist friends do not believe He even existed and argue that "Jesus" was a common name during this era.

I just know that this green-eyed lady and her daughter had their lives changed for the better. I believe "Jesus" was placed here on Earth by the Creator to teach humans the following message: Love, charity and forgiveness. The message is simple because humans are not the brightest animals on the planet. I believe we were placed on this tiny planet to help each other, not to destroy each other.

The Creator of the Universe is, was and will be. The power of the Creator is so massive, so overwhelming that we cannot as mere tiny humans fully understand the concept "GOD." The closest I can come to explaining "GOD" is to conceptualize energy, time, space, gravity and the speed of light in one. This unified force that created time and space is powerful enough to bring a child to this tiny planet. I believe Jesus did not come to Earth to care for the rich. We have attorneys, accountants and doctors. He came to save all of us from ourselves and for all of creation.

The disabled poor have lives that are so difficult, they need divine intervention to help carry their heavy cross of poverty and disability. I help take wheelchairs to poor, disabled people in other countries because

I know in my heart that is what the Creator wants ME to do. This is my path. Having personally experienced what life was like when I needed a wheelchair and no one but my ex-wife would help me, I understand the need.

Look up. Out there in our inner solar system there is no meaningful life. Study science and learn about how the universe really works. Study astronomy. It will help you get a true perspective about our tiny planet and why life here is so important. The nearest star system, Proxima Centuri, is at least 4.2 light years from our tiny home. The fact that there is life on our beautiful planet is itself a miracle. It's God's miracle.

Given that reality, ask "Why am I here? What is my purpose in life?" A life without purpose turns to various vices including alcohol, drugs and the lust for money.

After the distributions, we held a sports camp in downtown San Jose at a beautiful park. People were playing football, jogging, having picnics and some were playing tennis. The Costa Ricans were fit, obviously happy and enjoying their freedom. A few police were nearby just enjoying the sunshine and staying out of the way. The park had older facilities but an enthusiastic crowd. Some artists and food vendors were selling their wares.

We taught their athletes how to play wheelchair sports. We had about 30 athletes and many family members. We provided them with sports wheelchairs. There were so many disabled athletes, not everyone had a sports wheelchair. Some were trying to play wheelchair sports in everyday wheelchairs.

One of the recipients had a chair contributed by a friend in Salt Lake. Randy Curry, now deceased, was a quiet wheelchair tennis athlete who left the investment banking world to do social work. He gave me one of his expensive extra wheelchairs to provide it to someone that would put it to good use. This is how we get nice chairs. People in the U.S. contribute them to people in need in other countries.

A young lady who had a difficult time walking because of CP received the wheelchair. It was going to make her life a lot better as she could rest or go for longer distances than she could by attempting to walk.

Richard St. Denis had me instruct their players how to play tennis. I lined up the athletes and hit them tennis balls so I could assess their physical abilities. Like everywhere in the world, there are the natural athletes who basically train themselves. You can show them a shot one time and they instantly get it. Others are slow or have less ability.

It is important to hold a sports camp for the disabled after a distribution. A physical disability is not a life sentence or an excuse to never become part of society. Life is about what we can do, not what limitations we have because of poverty, or mental or physical health. We need to show people that a wheelchair will allow you more mobility, including playing sports. Many young men and women played sports before their life-changing disability. What sports does is improve mental health, as well as keeping the person in better physical shape. Having a disability is no reason to be out of shape.

A father and son were playing tennis in the court next to us. To their surprise and that of our disabled athletes, I asked them to join us for a game of doubles. We needed to show the disabled and their able-bodied countrymen that you can interact with people with disabilities. We need to rid the world of the stigma of disability. Having a wheelchair to get around is like taking your mountain bike everywhere you go. It's difficult but not impossible.

The father was in his early 40s. He and his 12-year-old son started hitting with us. They soon realized that athletes in sports wheelchairs can play sports, especially tennis. So they got into it and then we had a very competitive match. I don't remember who won, but Richard can't beat me, so I will say my team did.

Richard and I have been hitting tennis balls at each other since Brad Parks and Jeff Minnibraker invented the sport. The thing I do remember is the Costa Rican disabled players were interacting with the local population. Everyone was having fun.

One retired American was watching us play and volunteered to teach them tennis once a week. This tall, handsome, middle-aged black man retired from the military. He and thousands of Americans have retired in Costa Rica. He was excited to help others. The athletes were no longer perceived as pitiful. They were looked at as people in wheelchairs. There are people all over the world who will volunteer. When they ask to help out, welcome them. After the sports camp, we took the volunteers to the jungle to see the wildlife firsthand.

We went on a zipline adventure through the lush green jungle. None other than a Luis Quintana (unfortunately no relation) was the owner of a zipline adventure company. His workers were young healthy college students. Overhead there were flocks of blue and gold macaws. In the trees there were huge toucans. These immense black birds with their large gold beaks were quite the sight.

We cannot appreciate nature until we are in the thick of it with God's wonderful creatures. It's like listening to live music at a great venue versus your stereo. No matter how good your sound quality, it can't capture the moment or the music. The real world is an incredible place. You should turn off your televisions and visit it more often.

The workers and our volunteers carried us from the trails to the platforms. There we had help climbing on board the ziplines. A volunteer would travel ahead of us carrying our wheelchairs. We would follow and they would catch us at the bottom of the platforms. I had never experienced anything like it. The only word I have to describe this brief moment in time is "awesome." You are up on the canopy with birds and other life.

We next visited a coffee plantation. The bus full of volunteers stopped at the top of this incredible coffee plantation. The workers were from the poor surrounding countries. Like the United States, Costa Ricans live nice and their blue-collar work is done by immigrants from the poor countries next door.

While various nations can make a claim at the best red wine in the world, Costa Rica can give any nation a run for its money on coffee. The plantation reminded me of Napa Valley, California, where the vineyards are manicured. The restaurant at the top of the hill overlooking the vineyards had a couple of steps to get in and the bathrooms were not accessible. This is common everywhere.

The world is not going to become accessible because I am in a wheelchair. With help from our able-bodied friends, those of us in wheelchairs enjoyed the restaurant and the incredible views as well as world-class coffee. One T-shirt and a couple of pounds of coffee to take back to the United States, then we were off on our next ecotourism adventure.

River rafting through the jungle is always a wonderful way to appreciate nature. The following day, we went on a river trip through the jungle. There is something about howler monkeys screaming overhead. It is a sound you never quite forget. Different types of birds were flying above the river and into the trees. Insects and mosquitos were buzzing by our heads and looking for blood. The snakes remained hidden from view.

Seeing these wonderful creatures in the jungle in their natural environment works on every level. It's not as awful as watching them become mentally ill as environmental prisoners of war in a zoo where kids gawk at them and make faces.

Zoos serve their purpose because they help educate urban dwellers about the natural world. But ecotourism in Costa Rica is better on every level. Our boat pushed along with its seated passengers of able-bodied and those with disabilities. On the shores were giant copper-colored iguanas. I had never seen iguanas this large. It is not a good idea to swim, as the river has crocodiles. These crocs are not little creatures. They can easily rip a tourist to shreds. Fortunately, the snakes saw us before we saw them and they left us alone.

The young Costa Rican guide spoke in perfect English. He pointed out the various animals and what side of the boat to see the wildlife. He studied environmental science and tourism at one of this country's fine universities. A large number of Costa Ricans are bilingual and many have college educations. Their neighbors are poor, live in violent countries and do not have the rule of law. Without functioning legal systems, their societies suffer.

We saw a flock of critically endangered Roseate spoonbills. Their pink feathers made them look like flamingos. But their round beaks that looked like spoons at the end of their heads were a dead giveaway. If anything, these birds are proof the Creator has a terrific sense of humor. If this was in the United States, some nutjob would be shooting at them. The guide calmly told the tourists what animal or bird was where. The howler monkeys kept screaming their warning to the other creatures that humans were in the area.

I have never seen hummingbirds like the ones we saw next to a waterfall by the roads taking us up to the coffee plantations. These purple and green hummingbirds were 8 to 12 inches long and so beautiful it left you in awe at God's incredible creation.

Among our many volunteers were two young men in their early 20s from Colombia who were studying medicine. They were hugely helpful at every distribution. Their parents did not want them in Colombia with its then-violence and civil war with FARC. I asked the two why they were going into medicine. They stated they wanted to help people and improve their health. In the United States, often people go into the medical field to become multimillionaires, not to heal the sick. The sharp contrast in values between people in other countries and those of us entitled Americans never ceases to amaze me.

One thing is clear, tens of thousands of Americans travel all over the world doing humanitarian work. Despite the greed of a few misguided individuals, American humanitarian work does wonders for the world. Everywhere I have travelled in the developing world, I have met Americans already there doing humanitarian work. Americans do everything from building homes, schools, clean water systems, coral reef restoration, saving turtles to providing medical help.

Chapter Ten

I Hate America and It's All Your Fault

"Do not judge, and you will not be judged. Do not condemn, and you will not be condemned. Forgive and you will be forgiven"

Luke 6:37 NIV

Zip line in Costa Rica. The staff would bring the chairs so the disabled could zip line on their own.

On our second trip to Costa Rica, I arranged for television host Kimberly Perkins and her film crew to join us. Kimberly had a terrific humanitarian show called "Profiles in Caring". She is smart, adventurous and has filmed humanitarian work all over the world. Kimberly, her friend Jane and their cameraman Ken joined us on this distribution.

Kimberly and her husband Scott are successful. Nobody gave them a fortune. They earned their success. That success put them in a position to help others. When your cup is empty, you can complain but not help out. Kimberly and her friend Jane were there on their own dime. Theirs was true charity because it was from the heart. They did not have to help out Costa Rica's disabled.

Not everyone in Costa Rica is middle class. The immigrants from the poor countries next door are often destitute. Kimberly, her film crew and Lisa Murphy went to a shantytown outside of San Jose. As is often the case, not everyone that needs a wheelchair can make it to the distribution. Often, we have to take the wheelchairs to the homes of the disabled. They filmed the delivery of a wheelchair to a person in need who lived in a shanty. There were dirt floors, no running water and no electricity.

Many of the immigrants are illiterate but want to escape the grinding poverty and violence. There are the war refugees from Nicaragua, El Salvador or crime-ridden Honduras. Without the tens of thousands of poor immigrants, Costa Ricans would have to pick their own coffee, make their own beds, clean their own streets and they would have less crime. Their political problems with immigration mirror ours in the United States. The poverty in these other countries has deep American roots.

The Contras tried to overthrow the Sandinista Nicaragua regime. These American-trained and armed killers failed. So they turned to crime, everything from drug dealing and kidnapping to extortion. They have wrecked havoc on Central America. Without the poor immigrants and the crime from the Contras, Costa Rica would have a much higher standard of living.

Across the gullies will be middle class, nice suburbs. On the other side are shanties without running water, electricity and aluminum roofs for the newly arrived immigrants. It's like living in a nice neighborhood in San Diego and across the ravine is gut-wrenching poverty, no toilets, no running water and lean-to shanties. But the immigrants from the poor countries next door keep coming. Poverty pushes people out and economics pulls people in. This is the pattern all over the world.

We hired an immigrant driver named Hector to take us in his beat-up Volkswagen to the beach so we could film for Kimberley's show. I don't recall if he was from Honduras or Nicaragua. I just remember he was this ungrateful individual who drove slower than molasses through a straw. His poor driving was only exceeded by his ungrateful bad manners and terrible attitude.

On the way to the beach on Costa Rica's poorly maintained dirt roads, we had to stop. A migration of black and red crabs crossed the road. Traffic on both sides of this dirt road stopped, people got out of their vehicles and looked at the thousands of crabs crossing this country road. It was nice watching the respect the locals had for wildlife. In the United States, these crabs would have been road kill.

When we arrived at the beach, it was better than what I expected. The sand was black, probably from the volcanoes. I had never seen black sandy beaches. Hector waited patiently for us to finish filming as he smoked cigarette after cigarette. I don't know if he drank too much beer the night before or just fell out of bed and banged his head that morning. On the way back, he turned into a complete jerk.

As we are driving back, instead of taking the route that got us there in two hours, for some stupid reason he went on some back road. It got dangerous. At one point, Ken had to get out and guide us across this iron bridge. There were two heavy, but flimsy boards across this deep river. All I could think of was, I hope like hell this beat-up car makes it across this make-believe bridge. It's hard to swim with heavy braces and crutches. How are Kimberly and Jane going to get out from the backseat of this beater?

We made it across. I am the only one that speaks Spanish and had to listen to Hector talk the rest of the five-hour trip. It should have taken at most two hours to get back. I was stuck translating his crass remarks and getting more pissed at this trip that was taking forever.

By then, we were tired, sweaty and hungry. I had to hear how all of the world's problems are America's fault. I politely listened, translated and I would ask a question to try to point out his contradictions. Nothing I could have said or done would have mattered.

When you try to have rational discussions with irrational people, all you are going to get is aggravation. Never try to teach pigs to sing. If you do, you will only annoy the pig and get very bad music.

We were in Costa Rica doing a wheelchair distribution on our own dime and this angry "socialist" was denouncing our country. We are not responsible for American foreign policy decisions. We had nothing to do with the attempts by the any administration to overthrow the Sandinistas.

We are not there working for the American government. While politicians would not help out, that was not true of the American military. The U.S. Navy and our military always helps us with distributions.

We did not cause the flood of refugees trying to escape the violence of government-sponsored terrorism and the gangs that run entire countries next door. All we were doing was distributing wheelchairs, holding a sports camp for people with disabilities and showing our volunteers a terrific time with ecotourism.

His hatred of Americans was not justified. Numerous countries have lost wars. But, they have won the peace. Honduras has the same size population as Switzerland and approximately the same land area. The Swiss have one of the highest standards of living in the world. Their people are highly educated. You can do business with them because they respect the rule of law. I have friends who play wheelchair tennis from Switzerland. They are good athletes and work in a variety of professions. They are fun.

What Hector did not understand is the United States did not cause him to make his poor decisions. Our sponsors from Costa Rica were successful, well-educated, generous individuals. One was a doctor who accompanied us and spoke enough English to get by. He was furious at the immigrants who threw their garbage out their front yard and made no effort at education.

Unlike the Costa Ricans who were well-educated and bi-lingual, Hector only knew Spanish. Since his life was a wreck and he was poor, it had to be America's fault. It could not be his poor attitude, lack of ambition or other factors I knew nothing about. Hating Americans will not solve problems of poverty, crime and disability anywhere in the world.

Gabriela was one of our hosts. I was in Miami flying in on the way to play wheelchair tennis at the Florida Open. I ran into her at the airport. She gave me a huge hug and was happy to see me. She was studying business at an American university. Her wealthy parents' success made our wheelchair distribution possible.

When we do humanitarian work, don't expect everyone to be happy to see us. Many governments have made horrendous foreign policy mistakes. Yes, there are people all over the world who hate America,

Americans and others. Hate solves nothing. We are the little people, the commoners who are not responsible for the foreign policy of the rich people who run the planet.

Until poor countries choose the rule of law over crime and corruption, their standard of living will continue to be dismal. When you have to live in constant fear of being robbed, kidnapped and cannot even go out at night to a restaurant or enjoy a few moments by the beach, that is not the fault of the United States or other countries. This is the choice of the society in how they want their citizens to live.

There is no reason most developing countries don't take proper care of their disabled. I have played wheelchair tennis many times with my friends from Switzerland and other highly developed countries. They work as chemists, accountants, and in various other fields. Disability is not a death sentence in some countries. But the Swiss, the Japanese, the Germans don't have criminal gangs that will kill you for five dollars.

Americans get a bad rap worldwide. The American people were against the Vietnam war, the Iraq war and were against the support of military dictatorships. We just deliver wheelchairs to poor people. We don't care about their theology or their political beliefs. Poor people all over the world did not ask to be disabled. But if they need a wheelchair, we try to help them.

Costa Rica has attracted companies from all over the world. Intel and Siemens as well as other capitalist giants have plants in San Jose. The ecotourism works. Yes, Costa Rica does have flaws. They don't properly enforce their marine laws. Some of their criminals kill thousands of sharks and sell the fins to the Asian market. But they are still much better off than their neighbors.

Our Peace Corps has students over there working off their college loans and volunteers teaching English, building homes and doing various types of humanitarian work. Humanitarians work hard at making this planet a better place for everyone. While governments will continue to make mistakes involving war and peace, common people are generous and helpful.

If we want to make a difference in the lives of people all over the world, join the Peace Corps or do some other type of volunteer work with our church or the Rotary Club or some other organization. It's worth it. And don't let the Hectors of the world stop us from helping others. Haters are going to hate. Humor them and move on.

Chapter Eleven

The Temples of Thailand

"For physical training is of some value, but godliness has value for all things, holding promise for both the present life and the life to come."

1 Timothy 4:8 NIV

    I think every middle-class person on the planet should visit Thailand. Unlike other developing countries, Thailand was never colonized. Thai society is intact. Their people have a sense of identity with healthy self-esteem. Thai people are some of the most generous, warmest and fun-loving on our small planet.

    To understand or appreciate this ancient civilization, you have to "experience" Thailand. Their food, temples, elephant camps, shopping — this society is wonderful. Even their corruption, while at times annoying and often humorous, is tolerable.

Delta took us from San Francisco to Japan's Narita airport. There, we took the connecting flight to Seoul. We flew into Thailand on Korean Airlines. Bangkok has a beautiful modern airport. It's one of the many things you notice as you fly around our small planet, most countries have better, cleaner and more modern airports than our own old rundown infrastructure. Many of our airports were built in the '60s and '70s and it shows.

Next stop was the Catholic orphanage in Pattaya, a few miles south of Bangkok. The poor prostitutes give their children away to the Catholic Church. These poor children often have deformities, missing limbs or are otherwise not "perfect". They have the love of the nuns and the other children.

It's a short cab ride to the Catholic orphanage where we were being housed for this distribution and sports camp. I got there late and joined the team for breakfast. My sports wheelchair did not quite get there. Thai baggage handlers are just as capable of losing luggage as those in the United States. The next day, the airline brought my sports wheelchair to the orphanage.

Each morning before we went to the distribution site, we gathered for breakfast. Richard St. Denis would lay out the assignments for the day. We would discuss who was going to be with what team and then get on the half-hour bus ride to the sports facility outside of Pattaya.

The sports facility was built by a local contractor. In Thailand if you are the lowest bidder on a government contract, you can squeeze the project further and sell it to an even lower bidder. Consequently, the work will not always be to world standards. As we pushed our wheelchairs on the soft asphalt, it would tear up and leave marks as it was coming apart. They have a saying, "there is the right way and the Thai way." Despite the corruption, the society works.

The swimming pool was half full as the contractor got into a dispute with the city. But the facility functioned just fine for what we had to accomplish, distribute wheelchairs and host a sports camp for their disabled. This distribution was truly massive. I don't know how many wheelchairs we distributed, but it had to be several hundred.

The three tables were set up and the Thailand Rotary Club volunteers were there helping with every part of this humanitarian project. The Rotary volunteers were from all over the Western world. One volunteer was from Great Britain. This middle-aged, balding gentleman could work like nobody's business. He would unload chairs, bring over supplies, whatever was needed, he was there. That ole Brit and his very capable friends worked like it was his children he was helping. Whatever needed to be done got done.

The grant money from the Poulsbo Rotary Club in Poulsbo, Washington provided us a $30,000 grant that got the wheelchairs to Thailand. They also communicated with the Thai Pattaya Rotary Club and that is how we got their help.

The Thai people had their own volunteers and translators. I don't claim to know Buddhist culture. But from everything I saw, it works. The disabled are not shunned like in other countries and cultures I have visited. I think it is a Buddhist belief that your suffering in this life is retribution for sins in another life. You are given an opportunity to correct those wrongs in this life.

I would watch as abled-bodied Thai volunteers helped their disabled compatriots. They were kind and compassionate with their disabled relatives and friends. If someone was born with a deformity and their hands were missing, their friends would touch their stumps and interact with them.

After we unloaded the wheelchairs, the recipients arrived from various parts of the countryside and poor urban areas. Their government worked directly with the Mobility Project and identified people in need of wheelchairs. Since not everyone in Thailand has vehicles, relatives or friends brought some of them to the distribution. This is a common practice all over the world.

It was the usual setup for one of our distributions. The disabled poor would be placed in a common area with chairs for them to sit and wait their turn. They were given water or something else to drink to offset the hot humid Thai weather. While it is freezing cold in February in most parts of the United States, in southern Thailand it is hot and humid. It was like Florida in summer, hot, sweaty, but nice.

We saw every type of walking disability. The elderly needed wheelchairs and walkers because old age had worn out their body parts and affected their ability to walk. There were young workers who had been injured in traffic or work accidents. A few were there because of deformities resulting from birth defects. One thing was very clear, diabetes was not a major cause of their disabilities. Thai food is superior.

The Thai diet has to be one of the best in the world. At every street corner there is a vendor selling great food produced locally. In my opinion, the Thai are among the best cooks on our planet. Everywhere you go, the people are fit and happy. This will soon change. Numerous American fast food joints were opening. Having ruined the health of people in the United States, these fast food giants are intent on ruining the health of everyone on the planet. And they are succeeding.

As we were pushing our wheelchairs down the city streets, we passed one of Thailand's many fine stores and there in the window was a wheelchair for sale. Why were we there bringing wheelchairs to a country that has several billionaires, a modern airport, modern hotels, ecotourism and wonderful people?

We were there because the poor disabled people who need wheelchairs do not get them. When I look back at the distribution to Thailand, I often think, if we did not help, who would help their disabled poor? The reality is their poor and disabled have the same needs as others we help.

It's for the same reason we distribute wheelchairs to a rich country like Mexico. The poor are not going to be helped unless someone helps them. Unlike Costa Rica, it is not going to be Thai's wealthy that step up. We are there delivering wheelchairs to poor people because it must be done.

Clearly, the people who came to the distribution needed wheelchairs, walkers and our help. Some had very old, rusted chairs that were falling apart. Others did not have wheelchairs.

As we did in other countries on one of our many trips to the countryside, we took wheelchairs to people who could not make it to the distribution.

One middle-aged injured man and his family lived in a grass hut. The wife was caring for their children. The injured man was resting on a hammock. There were pigs running around with the chickens. The children were playing and laughing. The man was in obvious pain, lying in his bed. Lisa and I delivered him a nice wheelchair.

In addition to not having a wheelchair, his grass hut with its cement floor had steps. There was no ramp and no accessible bathroom. We got him into a wheelchair that was a perfect fit. Fortunately, this man did not have a pressure sore like some of the other individuals we wanted to help.

Some of the people who we provided wheelchairs had pressure sores. Without antibiotics, a pressure sore is a death sentence. After we helped them into their wheelchairs, we explain to families what would happen if a pressure sore is not treated.

A pressure sore is a skin break that happens when you bruise the skin, usually on the buttock region. The bones don't have muscles to relieve the pressure and the skin finally gives way. These sores become infected. The infection spreads rapidly and the person dies within weeks. I've had several wheelchair-using friends here in the United States die from infected pressure sores.

This is why if you are in a wheelchair, you have to raise yourself up every ten minutes or so if you do not have enough functioning back or leg muscles. Pressure sores are common for those with spinal cord injuries. We gave the families handouts that explained how to treat a pressure sore. We did this in every country we visited.

We explained to his lovely family that they needed to build him a ramp and an accessible toilet. The ramp was doable. A few pieces of wood, a saw, hammer and nails and he would be free to move around his small home and property. Now the accessible toilet — well, I had to use an outhouse when I was growing up on a small farm in Costilla, New Mexico. He would have to have his family build him an accessible outhouse.

How long would he live after his new shot at life? What would he do? That would be up to him and his family. There is opportunity for the Thai disabled poor. This is a very high-functioning society with a thriving middle class. There are many fine universities. The Thai economy has numerous Japanese industrial plants. It would not be too far of a stretch to view Thailand as an economic colony of Japan.

I met several very successful disabled individuals in Thailand. One was a world-class athlete who had won gold medals in racing in the Paralympics. Others were government employees or individuals who worked for non-profits that assisted us with the distributions and sports camps.

Thailand is not Afghanistan. Thousands of Americans have retired and live there. Millions of people from all over the world visit this incredible country. Their disabled who have ambition and the will to succeed often do.

One of the disabled athletes I met was Anna. She will always have a warm place in my heart. She is a young lady who was born without hands. When drugs are illegal in the United States, greedy companies sell these same drugs in other countries knowing full well they will cause birth defects. Thus, you see children with various disabilities caused by pregnant mothers taking drugs not allowed for sale here.

We taught Anna how to play tennis. She taught herself computer science and English. She was also getting her degree in business. As I was teaching tennis, I met Matt, a retired American. He sold his computer business and lives in Thailand with his Thai wife and children. He was playing tennis in the courts next to us and volunteered to help out. Matt was a good assistant and was interested in helping Thailand's disabled. Without pay and just wanting to make things better for others, he came every day and volunteered.

We taped the racket to Anna's arm and she had amazing coordination. In 30 minutes she was hitting perfect topspin from baseline to baseline. She and her friends picked up on the sport in a hurry. They were all high school students and were destined for success. Their attitudes were what was going to drive their success.

We had plenty of disabled Thai volunteers. They had their own wheelchairs and some needed an upgrade. We helped them and they helped us. Thai volunteers would assist with translation, placing their countrymen in wheelchairs or assisting with walkers, whatever was needed. They brought us great food every day.

In one of our sporting events, we had so many disabled athletes we held a relay race. We had four lines of disabled. Some were severely disabled, others could run like the wind and quite a few were competitive racers. We spread them out equally and let the fun begin. Everyone had a blast. The slow runners were competing against slow runners. When they finally finished their lap and passed on the baton to a faster runner, he or she would make up for the slow one. The volunteers joined in and it was the event of the day.

We invented a sport by dividing the camp into two groups. Each was given tennis rackets. Then we hit a tennis ball across the net to the other team. The goal was to keep the ball in play on your side. Then hit to the other side where, if the tennis ball stopped, your opponent scored a point. Since the courts were somewhat enclosed, if you hit it out of play it was also the other team's point. The able-bodied and disabled all joined in for the competition. Everyone played and had a great time. We did this tennis event all over the world.

After the all-day sports camp we would have dinner. At dinner we would sing karaoke. Some people should not sing and no amount of alcohol will change their voice for the better. The fact that some of the singers were so terrible, me included, is what made us all laugh.

When we do distributions, we often have inspirational talks with the disabled. We had several Paralympic athletics from the United States with us on one of our distributions. We were at an orphanage and our group included many individuals who could barely push their wheelchairs because of a variety of disabilities. My friend Rick Russo was with me. He has been in a wheelchair from a skiing accident for several decades. He is also an accomplished home designer and plays the guitar. Rick and I have fun on our various wheelchair distribution adventures.

As the athletes were talking to the young people about wheelchair sports and encouraging them to try to make the Paralympics, I looked at Rick and whispered, "this is really bad advice for these young people." He nodded and whispered, "they can barely move their chairs, much less compete in sports internationally."

I was asked my opinion. I decided to give the students my own advice. "Play sports to stay healthy and for enjoyment. But there is no future or money in wheelchair sports. This is the reality of life. Study math, science, business, engineering, but do not try to make a living by making your life goal a Paralympic gold medalist. Your education is your best chance at a decent future."

The Paralympic athletes looked at me in dismay. I was not there for them. I was in Thailand to help their disabled. Several of the students talked with me after and we discussed what they were studying. While young people should have dreams and aspirations, it is important to be realistic about ability as well as our disabilities. We cannot do anything we want if we set our minds to it. This concept is just ridiculous. Even when I was abled-bodied, I was never going to play in the N.F.L. or become a professional basketball player. I did not have the physical ability. Giving people false hope does not serve them.

One bright but frail student was good at math. I suggested science or engineering. He was thin, handsome but quite weak physically. He smiled at the thought of becoming a scientist.

I told him to keep working out. Being healthy is its own reward. These students listened. It was obvious they were going to be much better with their studies than with the goal of being an international wheelchair athlete.

One of Thailand's Paralympic athletics would have succeeded at anything he attempted. I think he had polio when he was young. But that did not stop him. He had the physical ability these other frail students lacked and was in excellent shape. After his success at racing in the Paralympics, he got a job, drove a nice truck and was always well dressed. His advice was "always try your hardest at whatever you do." That is advice all of us can follow.

Despite the paralysis of his skinny, polio-damaged legs, he had tremendous physical ability from the waist up. If he had gone into wheelchair tennis, he would have succeeded at an international level. He had amazing hand-eye coordination, was in great shape and had a positive attitude. Those are winning combinations in most parts of the world — and in sports.

As we were leaving Pattaya, Anna and her friend were seated on some stairs talking with me about life, sports, education and how much fun they had at the camp. Anna had tears as she loved what we were doing and was going to miss us. I gave her our best tennis racket. As the semitrailer was being loaded with sports chairs, wheelchairs and equipment a tennis ball fell out of one of the containers and rolled in front of us. "That is yours, too." Amazing things happen when we are doing what we are supposed to be doing. These little miracles happen to us all over the world.

In Chiang Mai, we had more of the same, poor people with disabilities being placed in wheelchairs. At this particular distribution, I thought we literally ran out of wheelchairs. There remained a cute couple with their little girl who needed a wheelchair. We were out, or so I thought. I look across the warehouse where we were holding the distribution and I saw something in the distant corner.

I pushed my chair over there and found a little purple wheelchair. I brought it over and it fit the little girl like a glove. It was perfect for her. It did not need any special adjustments or anything. It was what she and her family needed. Was it luck?

Jeff Murphy once told me, "there is no such thing as luck." He believes that if you are doing what you are supposed to be doing, the

Lord will provide you with the resources to carry out your task. These little "miracles" continue to amaze me all over the world.

I think humans have genetic memory. It seems to be passed on at conception through the DNA from one generation to the next. In many of my travels, I get this sense I have been here before. I did not get that feeling from Thailand. This was a completely new adventure and fresh memory. But this is one place I will always love and consider my home away from home. I encourage you to visit the temples, their tiger zoo, ride the elephants, go to the elephant show, the crocodile farm, shop at their incredible markets and enjoy one of the greatest countries and cultures on this small planet.

Part of the reason for their tremendous success was their now-deceased King Bhumibol Adulyadej, who looked like a nerd Thai version of Bill Gates. He was very well-educated and had an attention to detail that worked. He insisted on saving the elephants by putting them to work with ecotourism. People could now go for long elephant rides through the jungle.

After the jungle safari, the elephants would take you back to their camp and you would have lunch. Then the elephants would do this incredible show. They would play soccer and have a shoot-on goal. After the soccer shoot out, they would play darts. Then the elephants would paint beautiful paintings. I spent the $50 and still have that beautiful flower painting.

Before we left Thailand, we went shopping on "Walking Street". The shopping there was the best I had seen anywhere in the world. I bought a $4,000 handmade suit for about $250 U.S. I picked up numerous art pieces for our annual auction fundraiser and many items to give away as gifts. I have never seen better shopping anywhere in the world.

I was at Walking Street with Meeche White, the director of the National Ability Center, one of the most successful sports recreation disability organizations in the world. As middle-aged, homely overweight Europeans and Americans were there looking for young prostitutes, I would tell Meeche in jest, "geez, these young beautiful Thai women find bald, middle-aged, overweight men to be quite attractive." She smacked me in the arm. "Knock it off. They are disgusting old men who are taking advantage of their poverty." She was right.

This is common all over the world. Instead of using money for the Creator's intended purpose, these men sexually exploit poor people all over the world. The Thai government understands that they have a sex trade. Their prostitutes are protected. They are taught safe sex and routinely given physicals. This is not the case in other countries. But it is a trade that exists because of the poor choices of others.

We did a distribution the following year that was as successful. The two months I spent in Thailand gave me a completely different perspective of our small planet. If a poor country like Thailand can protect their elephants, educate their people and provide them with medical care, what is wrong with the United States? The Congressmen who object to the public having access to healthcare have government healthcare.

If you are in the United States, homeless and poor, you are far worse off than if you live in Thailand, Costa Rica and many other countries. Their families are still intact. Their elderly are not warehoused. Their grandparents take care of grandchildren while their children work. Grandparents are cared for by their sons and daughters and treated with respect.

It is inspiring to watch social events for their elderly at their large public parks. Their elderly would gather and play cards, socialize, eat food, listen to music and enjoy life. Our elderly are too often warehoused and forgotten.

Greedy relatives in the United States sometimes wait for their elderly to die so they can inherit their money and possessions. There are vicious family fights over who gets the house, the bank accounts, the stocks and all the while forget why they had parents. That was not Thailand.

I made lifelong friends in Thailand. Nuttha and her friends helped at every turn. Thailand's temples are etched in my memory forever. Their attention to detail in their art work causes you to pause and think how many hours were spent perfecting these structures. Then there is the gold, emerald and white marble temples as well as the smell of the burning incense and the sight of the monks in their orange robes praying. It works. God willing, one day we will once again visit this land and enjoy the sunshine, the temples, their beautiful people and rich culture.

Part Three
THE FUTURE OF DISABILITY

Chapter Twelve

Then Came the CRASH

"Put on the full armor of God so that you can take your stand against the Devil's schemes"

Ephesians 6:11 NIV

While "greed" may be good in the movies, it crashed the entire global economy in 2008. The Recession of 2008 occurred for obvious reasons. The unfunded $3 trillion Iraq war was a huge economic drain. Add completely irrational mortgages, massive fraud in the housing market, securities fraud and our greed created a global economic disaster. If you were paying attention, you could see it coming. Home prices doubled while wages remained flat. There was no way the housing market could support the fraudulently inflated prices.

In mid-September 2008, I was in Hilton Head playing wheelchair tennis. A very dangerous event occurred. I was talking with my financial analyst and long-time friend Mark Quayle. "Did you see what just happened? Bank-to-bank lending has come to a complete halt."

Mark has been working in the financial field for a couple of decades. "Yes, this is really scary." The financial system works on borrowing and spending. Companies don't have millions of dollars in cash in their accounts and neither do most banks. They all depend on the commercial paper market where companies make payroll, banks honor the checks and all is good with the world. But, when the financial system crashed, the banks stopped lending to other banks.

Millions of Americans stood to miss their paychecks. The reality of modern life in the United States is most families are three missed paychecks away from civil unrest. If the workers did not get paid, there would be riots in the streets.

Our financial system, while complex, is also quite fragile. And not just the United States but most developed countries are three missed paychecks from martial law. If workers don't get paid, they stop buying goods and services. Since 70 percent of the American economy is consumer spending, the entire economic engine stops. We don't know what happens if the economy completely grinds to a halt. We don't want to know.

The U.S. government had run the country and the entire global economy right into the ground. We had two unfunded wars and a massive recession. Millions of people were losing their homes. Unless there was an emergency infusion of money into the American financial system, it would collapse and it would take out the entire global economy. The American people and the world were being held hostage by the very people that caused the collapse. The same thing happened as a result of the pandemic.

Over the objections of millions of Americans, Congress bailed out the large banks. Henry Paulson, the former CEO of Goldman Sachs fame, engineered a bailout that started at $750 billion. When the American people almost rioted in the streets, he went back to Congress and the final bill ended up at over $826 billion.

The nonprofit sector had many small players who did not survive. In the resulting crash, millions of people lost their jobs, homes, life savings and quite a few killed themselves. The United States homeless population skyrocketed. The consumerism materialism model obviously failed. Like most non-profits, the Mobility Project did not get a bailout check. We were not too big to fail.

We had wheelchair distributions already underway and more were in the planning stage. But now, raising money for the Mobility Project came to a complete standstill. When the entire global economy is crashing down, we could not expect the American middle class to reach into their pockets and help people in other countries. Our donors were all members of small churches and concerned family and friends. The Mobility Project had always operated on a shoestring budget. Money was raised for each distribution. The volunteers paid their own way and the wheelchairs were donated, refurbished and we did the rest.

By 2009, the Mobility Project was on life support and running on fumes. Jeff worked in his own business. Lisa, Brock Moller and Jenny Smith were working full time for the Mobility Project. Steve Oliver had resigned and was working on his own project. He was bit by some bug while on a distribution to Ghana and died shortly thereafter. There was chaos.

By 2009, everything that could go wrong nationally did. There was financial scandal after scandal. The auto industry collapsed. General Motors filed bankruptcy. Our allies were also in deep recession. The entire global financial system was collapsing all around us.

By 2010 the Mobility Project shut down. Its collapse left a small void in the non-profit world. Poor people all over the world still needed wheelchairs. People in poor countries are injured, some become ill and others are the victims of violence. The Mobility Project would no longer be there to provide them with wheelchairs and now the need was greater than ever. The Middle East exploded in violence.

After the collapse of the global economy and the Mobility Project's death, Richard St. Denis, his wife at the time, Hazuki, Tito Bautista, Kiki Gonzales and Jose Manuel Castillo did not give up on the disabled in Mexico. Richard had already planned to branch off. We were excited for them and behind them the whole way. The World Access Project rose up like a phoenix from the ashes of the Mobility Project. Richard St. Denis and his committed crew organized and funded the World Access Project. Their base of operations is Mexico.

The needs of the disabled poor are easy for the wealthy and powerful to ignore. It is not their family members who lack medical treatment for mental illness or need a wheelchair and cannot afford these services and equipment.

We don't have to be a Christian to help others carry their cross. In fact, we don't have to help do anything for others. We can adopt the view that "as long as I get mine, to hell with everyone else."

There is in the financial world the law of diminishing returns. At a certain point, acquiring more wealth just means we are chasing our tail. Owning a 6,000-square-foot home with nine bedrooms and six baths and a massive yard just means more cleaning, maintenance and stress. The taxes and upkeep create work, not free time. Our possessions own us.

What some people do not understand: Nobody cares about what possessions we own. Money is a tool to do the Creator's work. Many money-hungry people have few friends. They have people who use them. They are prisoners of their wealth and live in golden cages, surrounded by high fences, security cameras, no one they can trust with their lives, and they also have many enemies. Possessions cannot love us back. Things can be lost, stolen or they break. Our best bet is use money to buy memories, not things. If we really want to find contentment in this life, use our wealth to do good in the world.

There are many rich families that spend the majority of their time working to help others and changing this world quietly. They don't stand on the street corners waving an orange flag, shouting, "Look at me. I do humanitarian work."

The World Access Project is successful because a handful of volunteers have refused to let the idea of helping the disabled just die. Richard St. Denis and his crew continue the work in Mexico and help us to deliver wheelchairs all over the world. It has become a way of life. They have made a big difference in the lives of many poor people and convinced the Mexican government to join in and help their disabled.

Today, the World Access Project works hand in hand with D.I.F., the Mexican government's social services agency. There are very wealthy individuals in Mexico who contribute money and equipment to them. The Rotary Club continues to help out and Mexico's growing economy is slowly pulling this country out of poverty.

After the Mobility Project ended, several non-profit organizations helped carry the cross of delivering mobility to the disabled poor. Hope Haven West is out of northern California. Jim and Carol Wilson help them. It is run by Lonny Davis, who, along with Jim and Carol, was on the board of directors of the Mobility Project. Hope Haven West collects and refurbishes wheelchairs and delivers them all over the world. They also work with the Rotary Club and have done a terrific job picking up where the Mobility Project finished.

Bree and Jeff Lair started volunteering for the Mobility Project in Mazatlan. Bree when on several distributions and after finishing therapy school, she now does nonprofit work doing exactly what she loves. Bree and her dad Jeff were always a big help. They formed PUSH International. Bree still works in Mexico doing physical therapy programs for children. They also are helped by the Mexican government. The work continues.

CHAPTER THIRTEEN

The World Access Project

"So neither he who plants nor he who waters is anything, but only God who makes things grow"

1 Corinthians 3:7 NIV

After Richard St. Denis adjusted to a permanent life on wheels, by chance he got involved in something that changed his life and the lives of thousands of people all over the world.

Richard was an Air Force mechanic and was stationed in Thailand prior to his accident. He was a Vietnam War-era veteran and was still in the service when he got injured. After his injury, he finished his education and became an attorney. While in Washington, he and other people with disabilities forced Congress to change disability laws.

A group of disabled veterans and other activists chained themselves around the White House and Newt Gingrich's home. They forced passage of the Americans with Disabilities Act (ADA). This change in the law made it mandatory that all public buildings be made accessible to people with disabilities. Simple things like curb cuts in sidewalks, accessible bathrooms, ramps into buildings — all was made possible by the ADA. Accessibility is now an accepted reality of public life. Reasonable accommodation is deemed reasonable.

Richard got involved in wheelchair distributions in 1997 when he was invited to Mexico by his pastor, Sam Talent. Richard was living in Colorado. Sam wanted him to talk to Mexico's disabled. Richard went to this tiny Mexican village located at 9,000 feet above sea level. Thirty people who attended the church are disabled and only one had a wheelchair. And that one was falling apart. Richard had taken an extra wheelchair with him.

A young woman named Leticia Lizande needed a wheelchair. She had been a shut-in her entire life. When Richard helped her get her first wheelchair, it changed her life and his forever. It fit her perfectly.

Prior to her wheelchair, Leticia's mother carried her from her bedroom to the other room in their tiny home. Her disability was a prison. She was not able to even get around in her yard or go down the street to the store. Her life was a living hell of constant suffering. The smile on her face and gratitude touched his heart. That is the power of love, the most powerful force in the universe. We have to experience love at least once in our life. God is LOVE.

To explain it, Richard quotes Mark Twain: "The two most important days in your life are when you are born and when you learn your purpose in life." (Rumor is Mark Twain did not really say that, but it sounds good. So, let's go with it). It certainly makes it easier to get up in the morning if we know why we are on this tiny planet.

Soon Richard started working delivering wheelchairs all over the world. When we are on the right path, the good Lord will find companions to join us on our journey. We meet the people we are supposed to meet when we are doing the Lord's work. Richard assembled a terrific team to take over the work of the Mobility Project in Mexico.

Jose Manuel Castillo — "Causti" — lost three limbs in an electrical fire. Both his legs were burned off. His left arm was cut off above the elbow and his right hand was badly burned. Causti still has his good humor, an incredible mind and prostheses. He walks on his artificial legs and in addition to his work with Richard, he and his lovely wife Rosa run a photography business. They shoot weddings, birthday parties, sporting events, you name it. Causti was the administrator for the World Access Project. Both his daughters graduated from college in Mexico.

Watching Causti do all of the paperwork with his one good hand and pleasant disposition was always a joy. We take our wheelchair recipients in front of the World Access Project banner, Causti takes their picture and on to the next person. Then Causti gives us the paperwork for our next rider, and the next and the next.

Enrique "Kiki" Gonzales was injured when he was 12. He fell off a tree and broke his back. He has worked with Richard from the beginning. Kiki does the mechanical work that he learned from Jim Wilson and Jeff Murphy. He learned how to repair wheelchairs. He also does the artwork for the organization, as well as selling his fine art privately. He can paint in various mediums and his freehand drawings bring art to life. Kiki is always smiling and is very pleasant to be around.

Tito Bautista joined wheelchair world when he was a young child. He contracted polio. He worked hard to get his college education. Later he became a world-class athlete and competed in the Paralympics representing Mexico. He is the sports director for the World Access Project and sets up their sporting events. He also translates and leads teams on wheelchair distributions. He is handy with tools and a natural leader.

Richard received the prestigious Heroes award from CNN for his humanitarian work. He and his crew have delivered thousands of wheelchairs, walkers, crutches and canes to poor Mexicans and in other countries in Central America. They hold an annual sports camp in Mazatlán.

Humanitarian work is an adventure in giving. It warms my heart every time a poor family says "gracias" and I get to see the smiles on their faces. When we make someone's life better and they are grateful, it does make us feel good. We share in their happiness.

Richard's lovely, talented ex-wife Hazuki speaks Japanese, Spanish and English. She runs her Christian school for people with disabilities and manages the teachers under her. She also helps with the distributions and does an outstanding job. She and Jose Manuel's lovely wife Rosa cook at the distributions and make things succeed.

Fast forward to today and the World Access Project is an established organization in Mexico. The Mexican government has changed its attitude about disability. Today, government social workers do a great job in helping with wheelchair distributions. They provide transportation and identify people in need. We provide the wheelchairs.

Why are we there?

Chapter Fourteen

Mexico Is Not a Poor Country

"Better a poor man whose walk is blameless than a fool whose lips are perverse"

Proverbs 19:1 NIV

There are millions of poor people in Mexico. But this is not a poor country. Mexico is the 11th-richest nation. As you drive by a marina in Puerto Vallarta or Mazatlán, you see multi-million dollar yachts in the harbor. Mexico has no shortage of millionaires and even billionaires. One of the richest men on the planet, Carlos Slim, is Mexican. This country is the third member of the North American Free Trade Agreement, NAFTA.

This treaty between the Canadians, the United States and Mexico created the largest economic bloc in the history of the world. NAFTA is approximately 22 percent of the global economy. With a combined gross domestic product (GDP) of over $21 trillion, this economic bloc vastly improved the living standards for millions of people. It also devastated small Mexican farmers and American workers in the midwest. At least 12 million indigenous Mexican farmers lost their livelihood to the tax-subsidized American mega-farms. After the farmers migrated to Mexico's booming cities, when jobs ran out there, they went north. But their poor would sometimes get injured and need wheelchairs.

My ex-girlfriend Bridgette and I were looking at a beautiful mega-yacht that had a helicopter pad and speed boats parked in the harbor at Puerto Vallarta. I looked at her and asked, "Why the hell are we delivering wheelchairs to this country when they have people who are this rich?" She looked at me, smiled and replied with her usual wisdom, "Just because a country has rich people does not mean they take proper care of their society. We are here because these people need wheelchairs."

It is fitting that super yachts are in the harbor as Puerto Vallarta is one of the most beautiful cities in the Western Hemisphere. The hotels and time shares are opulent, well-maintained and the service is exceptional. As we sat on the balcony overlooking the ocean at our beautiful condo drinking our coffee, I couldn't help but wonder why this government does not buy its people with disabilities wheelchairs. It just doesn't. But the government does help out.

This is not the Mexico of times past. With limited resources, Mexican social services government workers assist with the wheelchair distributions. Their workers are polite, caring and take us from our nice hotel to the distribution site, a local evangelical Christian church, DIF, as the department is called, does an outstanding job of providing help to the disabled poor, and does it with very limited resources. They depend on us to get the wheelchairs. We depend on them to get the poor, disabled people that need them. Two of their workers transported us to poor homes on their days off so everyone who needed a wheelchair or walker got one. They care about their poor, disabled citizens and it showed.

Like other parts of the developing world, the Grapevine Christian Church community is there to give people a hand up. This church has been helping us and is actively involved with the distributions.

Unlike other Central American governments, Mexico is climbing out of poverty. There are neighborhoods and hotels in Mexico that rival anything anywhere on Earth. The beaches and restaurants in Puerto Vallarta and other tourist cities can compete with the best anywhere. Mexico is the world's third-largest auto and truck producer. Their universities are excellent. Their workers have a strong work ethic. Over one million Americans have retired in Mexico.

Partido Revolucionario Institucional (PRI) controlled Mexico since the 1910 Mexican Revolution. This political party was amazing in its ability to stay in power. They have finally been voted out.

PRI made some huge economic mistakes that set back the standard of living of this beautiful country. They did not invest enough in public sector education early on. Their schools were not properly funded with teachers and supplies. They did not spend enough money on infrastructure. Their successors are quickly correcting those mistakes today.

The previous Mexican governments did not care. The children of politicians went to private schools or studied in the United States. The fact that the poor villages of the indigenous people remained poor, without adequate electricity, running water and paved roads, was not seen as their problem. Add racism and Mexico's upper class, almost all of whom are "sangre azul" — light-complexioned and very proud of their

Spanish heritage — and you have a caste system. The millions of poor, dark brown, indigenous natives struggle.

The caste system established by my Spanish conquistador ancestors remains in place here in Mexico. The ruling class is very European. The middle-class is comprised of mixed bloods. The vast numbers of poor are indigenous, dark-skinned natives. Near the bottom are the former black slaves. Further down the social ladder are the disabled. At the very bottom are the indigenous disabled.

Mexico has over 129 different languages from their vast indigenous populations. The Catholic Church saved the locals from total genocide and has a stranglehold on religion. In every village there is a Catholic church, a soccer field and a cantina.

The indigenous people are friendly and most are in reasonably good health. But that does not mean they don't have accidents, or illnesses.

Some estimates claim Mexico has over 4.1 million people who have some type of walking disability, out of a population of almost 130 million. Of these, about 45 percent live in poverty. Richard St Denis' estimate is that we need to provide at least 800,000 wheelchairs to the disabled poor in Mexico.

Yes, Mexico was attacked by the United States in 1845 and lost half its territory. But Germany and Japan also got their butts handed to them in the European and Asian tribal wars known as "World War II." They overcame defeat and today Germany and Japan have two of the world's most successful economies. These countries are clean, modern, very well run and their workers earn a nice living. Their citizens take vacations in Hawaii, Florida and we see them in Mexico.

Germany and Japan have auto plants here in this beautiful country. Mexico's beer industry has German roots. Mexico is not a "developing" country. It is fully developed but not everyone has shared in its success.

In fact, there are two Mexicos: first, the Mexico of the workers, the people, and the students. Then there is the Mexico of the upper class who live in gated communities and send their children to private schools.

Like every other human-created problem, Mexico clearly has the resources to provide for all of the health care, housing and educational needs of their young, growing population. Their upper class chooses not to. This is the situation worldwide with very few exceptions. Wheelchairs are very simple technology. Again, "If you can build a bicycle, you can build a wheelchair."

I have German and Japanese friends who play wheelchair tennis. They do not receive American aide for their disabled. While being disabled is still a social stigma in Germany and Japan, those societies take care of their disabled. My German friend Ellen Ellersblock is one of the best female wheelchair tennis players in the world. Japanese great Shingo Kunieda dominated men's wheelchair tennis until he got injured. He is still one of the best in the world. There are numerous great German and Japanese players. From top-ranked wheelchair tennis juniors to the No. 1 woman in the world, these two countries have done well.

Times change. Today, the Mexican government is competent, caring and works for its people. Many of the disabled in Mexico and various parts of the world are not seen by the tourists. The disabled are shut-ins, prisoners of their disability. Their relatives bring them food and care for them. But without a wheelchair or ramps or accessible homes, the disabled remain in the shadows, hidden away from the limelight. The Mexican social service workers are wonderful people who work hard to solve this problem of disability and lack of wheelchairs. They do care and help out. If they had more resources, they would do more.

Our wheelchair distributions bring hope to the hopeless. Often, the Mexican families are so poor they cannot bring their members to the distribution at the Christian church near the center of town in Puerto Vallarta. If the poor cannot make the distribution, then their government social workers and our volunteers load up their vehicles and take wheelchairs to those in need. You get to see how people really live. This is great fun. I enjoy these parts of the distributions.

The poor in Mexico have cement floors, running water and electricity. Their neighbors or relatives might have a car or truck. Everyone who can work does something to earn enough money to get by. The average wage in Mexico is $7.00 a day but the cost of living is at least twice that. Wealth is concentrated in very few hands. Paying workers a livable wage is a low priority for the Mexican upper class.

This is why Mexicans come to the United States. In fact, over 11,000,000 Mexican nationals live in the United States. They work at every type of job imaginable. From dishwashers to framers, to roofers, field workers, cement finishers, carpenters, plumbers, electricians, nurses, gardeners — name a job and some Mexican migrant is willing doing it. Because their work ethic is strong and they are honest, their labor is always in high demand.

The immigrants send money back to Mexico to their poor relatives. This money enables their elderly parents to survive and young children to obtain an education. What the immigrants cannot get is proper work visas. Citizenship is simply out of the question.

When a worker's parent dies or a family member is having a wedding, they cannot go home. If an immigrant leaves the United States for any reason, he or she cannot come back unless and until obtaining a valid visa. Since the U.S. government controls the visa process, they refuse to fix this corrupt system. There is a 14-year wait to enter the United States legally.

Mexico is the target of political venom. But Canadians, Europeans, Asians, Africans all have "illegal" workers in the United States. This convenient lie enables companies to exploit workers.

According to my clients who have migrated to the United States without permission, prior to the present always-corrupt system, migrants would simply hand a Mexican security guard $200. He would give the Americans $100 and they would go back to playing cards. Today, it costs $6 to $10,000 to bring someone across the desert in very dangerous conditions, with criminal gangs providing the immigration service.

When the workers are here in the United States working the dangerous dirty jobs U.S. citizens just won't do, they get injured and some die. If they are injured here, at times the employer has worker compensation insurance and the worker gets a wheelchair and small compensation.

Some of the people who get wheelchairs cause their own disability. Poor diet is a choice. At least one-third of the wheelchairs we give away at our distributions in Mexico are to people who have lost a limb to diabetes. It's sad to see otherwise healthy people who are amputees because of poor food choices. Hopefully Mexico's people will wise up, eat healthier and kick out America's food and drink giants.

Executives knows their products are causing a public health crisis with their sugar-saturated soft drinks in Mexico. They don't care. Then their plastic bottles end up in the ocean. As long as soft drink companies make more money this quarter than the last quarter, the plastic bottle pollution and the diabetes they cause with their sugar-saturated drinks are not their problem. Rich American companies don't help with the wheelchair distributions despite the fact that their food products and sugar-saturated drinks cause diabetes.

With help from the Mexican government and Christian volunteers, the World Access Project's wheelchair distributions are well-run. The Christian church at the particular city where we do these distributions provides the venue. Then volunteers fly down from the United States and Canada and other parts of Mexico and help the disabled get the items they need to provide them with more liberty.

We explain to their families how to use the wheelchairs and show them how the brakes work, how to fold them and other specific instructions on use. I always tease my recipients and tell them, "Don't go snow skiing in your wheelchair. No diving in the oceans, and do not assist the narco gangs by doing drive-by shootings. But you can go dancing with your new wheels."

One 93-year-old Aztec man was very gloomy and depressed. He had this look like someone just ran over his dog. He was suffering from dementia and was a bit senile. To cheer him up, I introduced myself as "Senor, yo soy el Presidente de Mexico, Benito Juarez." His eyes lit up and he immediately smiled. "Mucho gusto, Senor Presidente." He was shaking my hand and was ecstatic to finally meet me. He probably went back to his village and told all of his friends and relatives that he was just presented with a wheelchair by Mexican President Benito Juarez. My crew burst out laughing. Maybe in another life I was Presidente Benito Juarez. I don't know. He was happy.

It is important to have fun with these distributions. There is no reason for anyone anywhere to go without a wheelchair when people in the United States throw away thousands of wheelchairs each month. What we have is a logistical problem with people who need wheelchairs in one country and a spoiled entitled society that just throws away a piece of equipment that can be used by someone else in some other part of the world.

Mexico's economy will continue to grow. The people work hard, they are smart and you can do business with them because they keep their word. The country is dynamic with beautiful beaches, great food and wonderful people.

Chapter Fifteen

The Wheelchairs for Haiti Project

"Each man should give what he decided in his heart to give, not reluctantly or under compulsion, for God loves a cheerful giver."

2 Corinthians 9:7 NIV

In 2010, the poorest country in the Western Hemisphere had a massive earthquake. Over 20,000 people died. Tens of thousands more were injured. Haiti is one of the poorest countries on Earth.

This former French colony was the world's first slave society to throw off the chains of oppression and gain freedom. Haiti was France's richest colony. It was a major sugar and cotton producer. The French, English and Americans were terrified of a free, black former slave country. The United States refused to recognize Haiti. What could be done with free black people? The slaves could revolt and kill the masters.

Well, that was more than 200 years ago. Once Haiti won its freedom, the former imperial powers decided to strangle this free black baby in the cradle. A successful Haiti would mean the freedom of slaves and presented a clear threat to the United States' slave owners and the other European powers.

Add deforestation, lack of modern infrastructure, garbage collection, enough water treatment plants, sewage systems and you have a country where foreign aid is the largest source of government revenue. This poor country was not prepared for what happened next. They were already suffering corrupt government and poverty wages along with high unemployment.

When earthquakes, hurricanes, tornadoes or other natural disasters happen in the United States, our building standards are such that all of our structures are not going to fall apart. This is not the case in poor countries. If there is an earthquake in a poor country, adobe structures quickly fall apart. Anyone inside will be trapped and if not immediately killed, they will be injured and need wheelchairs.

As I was working out and looking at the television, the screen filled with shocking pictures of a massive humanitarian disaster. I called up

Lisa and Jeff Murphy. "Let's get these folks wheelchairs. Have you seen the pictures? This is horrific. Looks like the country has fallen apart."

Some humanitarian workers from Haiti contacted us. In the humanitarian world, we work together and often know each other. We coordinate projects with other organizations and are results-oriented. A very nice Haitian doctor who was on the ground in Haiti contacted us. Dr. Jean Baptiste was already there working with American volunteers.

We figured we could get them 200 wheelchairs. But it was going to cost at least $3,000. Before the 2008 recession, fund raising was difficult but not impossible. Except for the people that caused the economy to collapse, everyone was hurting. Our ability to raise money had dried up. We did a fundraiser and raised the money anyway.

If people have a negative opinion of the U.S. military, they need to get over it. These young men and women have helped us deliver wheelchairs all over the world. Lisa contacted the U.S. Navy's humanitarian Project Hand Clasp, based out of San Diego, and enlisted their help. We would have to get the wheelchairs to them. Our volunteers in Haiti would do the rest.

Lisa was once again successful in getting Hope Haven to get us wheelchairs. Soon we had most of what we needed, except our own people on the ground. Through networking, word got around. We had volunteers on the ground that could get the wheelchairs to the disabled. We had everything except a functioning Haitian government. Customs kept trying to steal the wheelchairs. Just as we had done in Nicaragua, we refused to pay the bribes and eventually our wheelchairs got there.

Our team did not go to Haiti. The country was destroyed. The last thing they needed was me, a disabled American, trying to be helpful but needing help because of my wheelchair. It was also too dangerous to send our crew that normally goes anywhere. We had to rely on the NGOs on the ground and Haitian volunteers.

We have no idea if the wheelchairs actually got to the people that needed them. We took our Haitian volunteers at their word. We did what we could from the United States. We have no idea if the people who received the wheelchairs are still alive. But we had to try something. It is easy to watch and let the world go by as others have hardship and do nothing. We can take the view that self-interest is the national interest. That attitude does not work in the humanitarian field. We are not there for ourselves. We are there to serve others.

There are arguments among intelligent people that perhaps sometimes doing nothing is the right thing to do. Is it better to send food to people who are starving and keep them alive and then have a 50 year problem of finding them employment, housing, medical care and access to legal services? What if we let the suffering people figure it out themselves? The answer is NO!

In an interconnected world where everyone is 22 hours by jet travel from every major city, doing nothing is a very bad idea. We live on a small planet. The fact that we live here in the developed world in first class means nothing.

It is like there is a fire on a cruise ship and it is in the lower deck. "Well, we don't have to be concerned about that." Really? Do people in first class in the developed world think that because the fire is in the lower deck "where those people live" it is not going to spread? Life on a very small planet is not quite that simple with a world connected by more than 80,000 flights each day. Bad news, health problems and fires spread quickly. And as we have learned, so do viruses.

There are tens of thousands of Haitian refugees who live, work and study in the United States, just as there are millions of workers here from all over the world. They all have relatives. Not helping a poor family on the other side of the planet or in our own hemisphere will create resentment. Those in need will remember that we could have helped but chose not to.

Haiti does not have to be a poor country. Poverty is a state of mind and a behavior. Going back to our standard example of how to run a successful society, Switzerland is not poor. Their people speak four languages, are financially competent and honest in their business dealings. Their country is spotlessly clean. The Swiss are among the best-educated people on the planet.

How can Haiti turn it around? Rwanda turned it around after the holocaust. This slave republic that won its freedom two centuries ago is once again on the edge of civil war. Haitians are actually going hungry. Their lives are a destitute nightmare.

Only Haitians can solve Haiti's economic, social and criminal lawlessness problems. The West cannot lift this country out of poverty. What is required to turn Haiti around is great leadership. I believe what Haitians need is a Golda Meir, Nelson Mandela, a Gandhi, an Oscar

Arias, a Paul Kagame, a leader who is above reproach and loves his or her people.

If Haiti wants to rise up out of the ashes of poverty, the people will need a leader who is fearless, honest, and well-educated. They will need extensive infrastructure repairs and good garbage service. They can do this. Haitians are some of the sweetest, most wonderful hardworking people you will ever meet.

Forests will need to be replanted, probably convert their educational system to either Spanish and/or English as the neighbors do not speak French or Creole. Haiti will need their diaspora to return and start small and big businesses. They will need to create products to sell in the world market and compete with the best of the best.

Japan, Germany and Rwanda have all risen like phoenixes from the flames of war and destruction. Obviously, it can be done. Success is possible, it just takes a change in attitude.

What I believe the United States should do to help pull Haiti out of poverty is let more of their wonderful people migrate and succeed. Then they will work with their relatives and rebuild this ecologically destroyed country. The Haitian government has to understand, what they are doing with drug dealing and rampant corruption is not going to work forever.

Chapter Sixteen

Sao Tome- Slaves Were Processed Here

"One man pretends to be rich, yet has nothing; another pretends to be poor, yet has great wealth"

Proverbs 13:7 NIV

There are places on this planet that are so beautiful, isolated and unknown that the fingerprints of paradise remain. Sao Tome Principe is this beautiful tiny island nation of fewer than 300,000 people just off the coast of Nigeria on the equator.

The tropical island was empty of humans until my Portuguese ancestors discovered it during their slave-trading days. Then my Portuguese ancestors turned this beautiful island to a processing center for the slaves who would be sold in Brazil, the Caribbean and the plantations of the Southern United States.

Lisa Murphy was contacted by Ned Silegman, and his organization Step Up. He is a disabled American ex pat who retired on this tiny island nation. We were told the small island nation needed about 100 wheelchairs, walkers, crutches and peddle carts. After securing the necessary wheelchairs and supplies, Lisa made our travel arrangements. Our flight would take us from the United States to Lisbon, Portugal. This trip involved four of us. Brad Moore is a strong and pleasant-to-be-around volunteer. Jeff and Lisa Murphy led the way. They made sure we were properly prepared, as they had for the previous, numerous distributions they'd organized all over the world. They had been there on a distribution previously and knew people on that island. The Rotary Club helped fund the distributions.

There are no direct flights from the United States to this former Portuguese colony. We stayed in Lisbon at a nice hotel with a good restaurant. It was my drinking year so Brad and I had some Portuguese red wine. The French, Spanish, Italians, Argentines and Californians have nothing on the Portuguese when it comes to delicious red wine. It is just better. The next day we packed our small carry-on luggage and boarded the large white jet, which had no markings, to make the long trip.

To get to Sao Tome, you have to fly from Lisbon down the center of Africa. The flight takes eight very long hours. We stopped in Uganda to refuel. From there, we flew into a single runway airport that was in surprisingly good shape. As we landed, we were not alone. We watched expensive corporate jets land. They had rich, well-dressed white boys carrying suitcases.

This country is not a drug haven and does not have the stench and bad attitude of drug dealers. Instead they have international banks. I looked at my friends and started laughing. "Cacao is quite valuable." Obviously, these rich boys were laundering money for their wealthy clients in Europe and the United States. Sao Tome has seven international banks, yet their only export is cacao. But, not our circus, not our monkeys. The super-rich have wealth that transcends national borders.

We were there to do a wheelchair distribution and a sports camp for their disabled. What the super-rich do with their immense wealth is between them and the Creator. We are humanitarian workers, not tax collectors or law enforcement. But it was amusing to watch the super-rich at work. Our calling was to meet the needs of this small island's disabled population.

The island has a lush rain forest, plenty of fish offshore, cacao and 300,000 poor people who all appear to be very healthy. In fact, these were the healthiest people I had seen anywhere in the world. The men and women had this incredible natural beauty. They walked almost everywhere and, without processed sugars, and eating natural foods, their bodies were fit. The people looked very happy. They had amazing smiles.

Lisa was enchanted by the beauty as we watched mothers washing their clothes in the small river that led to the ocean across the road. The young children were running, playing and enjoying a beautiful life of great health, love and good food.

Our host was named Danny. He is a nice young man who was housekeeping for Ned, our American ex-pat who found us on the internet. Ned's comfortable residence is next to the airport. It is a wheelchair-accessible house that has a pier out to the Atlantic. His comfortable home had everything for us to enjoy our stay. Danny and his girlfriend were there to show us around and help with the distribution. Next to the house was a chicken coop.

The rooster did not understand sunrise was not at 3:00 a.m. I nicknamed him "Drumstick." I had my plans to kill him in the middle of the night. Then we could get a good night's sleep. Every morning at 3:00 a.m., long before the sun was coming up, Drumstick would wake the world with his Sao Tome's "cockadoodledo." Since I was a guest in another country, I let him live. If I killed him, I would have to gut and clean him. That would be too messy.

In the street next to Ned's house, pigs ran loose, as did the neighbor's chickens and a few goats. Off shore in the early morning, you see local fishermen catching today's dinner.

The roads in the town are paved. The streets are full of people walking, with statuesque women carrying various items on their heads. The women wear colorful clothes that are made locally.

The locals live on a high-protein fish diet, fresh fruit, chicken and pigs. The other thing I noticed, this country is going to have a huge population explosion. Their young population does not practice enough birth control. Most of the young women of child-bearing age were pregnant.

On the way to town, we saw numerous businesses run out of people's homes. Want to open a tire shop? Stack the tires in front of your home next to the main drag and start selling them. The old tires are there waiting to pollute the local environment. The new tires or new used tires are waiting to be installed.

Are you hungry? Home after home have patios and a sign that they are more than willing to cook for you.

Need a massage? The sign says "Massage". Go in and get a massage. Since the homes were not wheelchair-accessible and we were there to do a distribution, none of us stopped and supported the local businesses.

Few people have automobiles or trucks. The impression that stood out the most in my mind is money does not buy happiness. The poor people of Sao Tome were some of the happiest I had seen anywhere on this small planet.

Ned was in Washington and not available to guide us or help with the distribution. There was a local government worker assigned to help us. She might show up or she might not. She was consistently late. The work got done despite her lack of effort.

We had a disability advocate who was one of our volunteers. He was very serious about his work. He had polio and uses crutches to hop around. His small, clean two-room office was the disability center.

The office had a desk, an old chair and an antiquated typewriter. There were a couple of disabled individuals that used braces, crutches or they just limped along. Each disabled person has a story. I never ask how they became part of disability world. Some were obviously born into disability world, others fell, were hit by a car, a few got sick. Unlike other parts of the world, I did not see one person who was disabled because they were shot or had their legs blown off by a First World land mine. We did not care how they got disabled.

We were next to the ocean and loved it. The blue waves with their white caps crash onto the white sandy beach. The large black rocks crawl up from the water and support the hotel's restaurant and balcony as it looks out over the peaceful Atlantic Ocean. The sunsets were beyond spectacular. They were unlike any I had seen anywhere in the world. Maybe it was because we were so close to the equator and the Atlantic was showing its best. The sea was a silver blue and the sky had the various orange, purple, pink and red hues of color with white and grey clouds as if God was showing us what true art looked like.

Our dinner was fresh fish caught that day. We were the only guests in the restaurant. The cooks grilled our fish to perfection. The balcony overlooking the ocean combined with the smell of the saltwater complimented the sound of the waves crashing on the rocks.

After resting and catching up on our sleep, we drove into town. In the harbor there were rusted ships that never made it back out to sea. They stuck halfway out of the water from the shallow harbor. They must have gotten grounded. The boardwalk was beat up from tropical weather and lack of maintenance. The concrete was cracked, the walls and railings were falling apart.

When we got to town, there was a plaza with dozens of taxis but no passengers that needed a ride. The men sat around, unemployed and broke.

A young boy approached our car with his hand out begging. He clearly was well fed. He was somewhat clean and looked to be about eight years old. His purple shirt with the holes, no shoes and torn pants provided the perfect picture for someone who can look into your eyes and ask for money. One day this child will grow up to be a politician.

The buildings in town were falling apart. Without the necessary paint and new cement, the balconies did not look safe. We drove to a section of town where there were several restaurants all clumped together. The plastic chairs were by fold-out tables. That atmosphere is enough for the locals. There were a few customers here and there. My guess is the poverty is such that most people just eat at home. Nobody goes hungry.

After dinner, we drove around the small city. The international banks are the most modern buildings in the country. There are armed guards outside. They look more bored than tough. If you rob the place, where are you going to go? The island is tiny and 200 miles off the coast of Nigeria.

The following day, I joined Danny on a trip to their mountains. Everybody else wanted to rest. I was restless and adventurous. Danny took me to their mountain volcano that rises above the rain forest. We drove up the old dirt road that led to a modern hotel.

As I was guiding my wheelchair through the thick grass, I almost ran over a dead snake. As I got closer, the snake had been cut in half. It was green and yellow. I moved it with a stick and left it at that. If there is one, they have family. Snakes and wheelchairs don't mix. I kept going.

The hotel at the end of the road had a guest from northern Europe. He was there on a diving expedition. Ecotourism provides this small country with much-needed revenue. On the way back to our guesthouse, Danny took me to where my Portuguese ancestors housed and processed slaves prior to taking them to the New World. It was haunting.

The place gave me a very eerie feeling. In the back of my mind, the large double-story buildings looked familiar. I could picture the slaves walking outside. I don't know how my ancestors did it, but they did. Guns must have played a big role as they were clearly outnumbered by the slaves. Kill one, scare 10,000. The place had this ugly feel about it that made me very uncomfortable. I don't know if it was the ghosts of a prior life or what. It was spooky. I did not like it. I could picture the slaves in chains and men with guns.

The next day we started our distribution. One of our volunteers was a national football star. This young athlete was there to help out of sheer kindness. He was strong and had a great laugh. The other volunteers and the recipients were all happy to see him. He did not flaunt his celebrity. He helped unload the chairs, crutches and set up the handcarts. That athlete was all work. With Brad and Jeff, things moved along at a good pace.

We had brought plenty of wheelchairs, and a few push handcarts, PETs. These Personal Energy Transportation handcarts had hand pedals for paraplegics. With someone who is able-bodied, they would have the pedals for the feet. Since a para's legs don't quite work, the hand pedals will do the job. What happens next is the person who gets this small wooden handcart now has a portable store. Instead of begging, the poor disabled person can sell flowers, deliver goods or just help their family by carrying everything from groceries to small children.

The distribution was covered by the local television station. Since there is only one station, we were instant overnight temporary celebrities. Lisa did some interviews and the locals were excited to get their wheelchairs, PETs and crutches. Then we did something we rarely do, we gave clothes away. This is a humanitarian practice I would like to end.

I am not a fan of delivering clothes to Third World countries as doing this generous act destroys their local clothing industries. The developing world is fast losing its indigenous cultures. Clothes are unique to each part of the world. With mass production, beautiful colorful local clothes are replaced by Kobe Bryant jerseys and blue jeans. Regardless, the locals loved the clothes.

I had brought an everyday chair that could be made into a sports chair. I gave that chair to one of the wheelchair athletes so he could continue to play sports and just have a much better chair. The old man was in his late 50s or early 60s, slim and had a nice attitude. The chair fit him perfectly.

Some of the people were missing limbs. One man had lost his leg in an industrial accident. His wife and relatives brought him to the distribution. We got him crutches for walking and a wheelchair for pushing in his house at night.

A young Portuguese woman was on the island doing humanitarian work. She came and said hello. She was there teaching sewing to the locals. She had started a small business for the women who live in the mountain villages near the city. On her own dime, she was there making life better for people she did not know. We have met people like this young lady all over the world. She gave me confidence in my belief that there are more good people than bad and we can all make a difference. We just have to choose to get involved and be participants in the game of life.

The next day after the distribution, we went to a local hotel and asked them if I could teach their local disabled population wheelchair sports. The hotel owner was a middle-aged lady who was reluctant to let the town cripples out on their one tennis court. I explained to her that she was going to be interviewed by the television station. It would be good for her business. She agreed and we set up our players in their sport and everyday chairs.

Like people all over the world, the disabled athletes wanted to play football. But, since they could not kick — either because they were missing limbs or worse, were paralyzed from either an accident or disease — we played a game of wheelchair soccer. We had a goalie and divided the players into two teams. You can carry the ball on your lap but have to bounce it. The goalies were intent on blocking shots. They loved it.

I knew that none of these players would ever have the opportunity to play tennis again. I invented a game called tennis war. It was going to rain so we hurried and divided the players in two teams. We gave all of them a tennis racket and told them that the goal of this game is to hit the person on the other side of the net. I told the players to protect their eyes and faces. Then the tennis war began. They were laughing as they tried to hit each other. Without serious injuries, we gathered our things as the rain was starting to come down hard.

When you are in the tropics, it rains a lot and it rains hard. We got everything put away and barely avoided getting drenched. A local restaurant donated the food and we had a nice meal with the athletes. We shook hands with all of the players, took lots of pictures with their permission and everyone left with a good vibe.

The next day we visited a couple of schools. To our surprise, there were U.S. Marines and Navy construction crews painting the schools. What people do not understand about our great military is that, in addition to keeping the peace, they do humanitarian work all over the world. They make life better for thousands of communities.

That evening we had just finished eating dinner and a local fisherman brought by the largest lobster I had ever seen in my life. He wanted $35 U.S. and I had no desire to kill that magnificent creature. We had eaten and there was no reason to kill this animal. In retrospect, what I should have done was bought that lobster and then set him loose at the end of the pier. I didn't and missed out on an opportunity to save an ocean elder. Lobsters can live for many decades. Constantly killing the sea creatures because we can is a bad idea by any measure.

We would see the fishermen bright and early every morning. They would be out in their small boats catching what they needed to eat or could sell at the local market, while leaving the rest of the fish for tomorrow. They did not waste seafood or kill animals for sport.

The locals made use of everything. A plane that could no longer fly was converted into a motel and restaurant. Nothing was wasted. I think people have a complete misunderstanding of what it is to be "poor." Poverty is a state of mind. You are as poor as your attitude. Great health, sunshine, family and friends, that is true wealth.

We went by a sports stadium. The locals were playing football. They were wearing sportsware with American icons like Michael Jordan and others. Their music was American but they speak Portuguese. I was not aware of any indigenous languages being spoken.

The locals were the descendants of slaves from the continent a mere 200 miles away. Since the island was uninhabited, the Portuguese and the slaves were the new arrivals and had been there for over 300 years. Portuguese became the default language as the slaves were from many different tribes. They all saw themselves as Sao Tome citizens.

At dinner one night, I was talking with a couple of the locals. A young man named George had been educated in the United States. He was well read. I could tell that one day he was going to be a leader in business or government. We talked about Patrice Lumumba, the brilliant leader of the Congo who had been murdered by the CIA. Lumumba could have done so much for that troubled country. Instead, our misguided policy at the time caused millions to die.

Sao Tome won its independence from Portugal in 1975. Danny related a story that before the Portuguese left they massacred hundreds of locals. They won their independence nonetheless.

This island paradise might survive. The international banks didn't appear to do anything for the local population. The infrastructure in the city is falling apart. The locals survive off the food they grow, the pigs and chickens they raise and the fish from off shore. The sad part is this peaceful way of life will soon be gone. They do well despite their lack of government, not because of it.

The discovery of oil offshore is going to destroy this island paradise. Then there are the large fishing trawlers from China, the European Union and Russia that can empty out a fishery with their massive nets. These ocean-killing machines are fishing out the fisheries all over the world. In Africa, local government officials can be bribed or the fishing is just done illegally. These countries don't have the naval resources to stop pirate fishing.

Today, half of the wildlife in the oceans is gone. At least 90 percent of the predator fish have been killed off. The Asians are slaughtering over 200,000 sharks each day for shark fin soup. And half of the coral reefs have been damaged or destroyed. When the oceans are fished out and the population of this small nation explodes, the poor planning of this banker paradise will result in a troubled future.

We don't have to fish out the oceans, kill the sharks and bring children to Earth we cannot support. Sao Tome citizens sell cacao and banking services. But they don't need anything since they have everything.

Countries like Sao Tome are the canaries in the coal mines. As these countries' resources are exploited, their populations explode and their leaders are bought off, they will lose not just their freedom. They will lose their entire peaceful way of life.

As we were leaving, we saw more young U.S. Navy men and women doing construction work at the nation's only airport. In addition to providing plumbing for their schools, and painting the buildings, they were also building a security fence for the airport.

We got up at 4:00 a.m. to catch our 7:00 a.m. flight. Ned's house was ten minutes from the airport. Getting up early was a complete waste of sleep. The plane was six hours late. As we flew off and I could see that beautiful island nation in the distance. I looked up at the sky. The sun was shining through the clouds and I saw the pier connected to Ned's house.

This trip was an adventure in humanitarian work. I said a small prayer thanking God for this opportunity to serve. Over 100 people got wheelchairs, crutches, handcarts, tennis rackets and smiles. We got great memories and the gratitude of some very happy disabled people who live in an island paradise.

Chapter Seventeen

Rwanda Overcomes the Genocide

"The desert and the parched land will be glad, the wilderness will rejoice and blossom."

Isiah 35:1ª NIV

Rwanda is a small country of 12 million people near the equator in the heart and soul of Africa. The genocide that took place in 1994 is the textbook example of the failure of local and international institutions. The madness of men with hate in their hearts almost destroyed this beautiful tropical nation.

November 2010. Lisa and Jeff Murphy and I were having dinner in Kigali with our Rwandan volunteers. One of them, Richard, had lost an arm in the genocide. As we were talking about the killings, tears came to his eyes. "We did this to ourselves. These were our neighbors, our babysitters, our cousins, our friends. What was wrong with us that someone on the radio three hours away could preach such hate and we would follow them?"

The airport in Kigali is modern. The streets of the capital are clean. The traffic lights work. The internet is First World quality. There is a master plan for the capital city.

We stayed at a very modern family hotel that was nicer than anything in Europe we had slept in on our trips to Africa. The staff at the hotel was courteous, alert and fluent in English, French and Rwandan. There was construction of beautiful homes across from the hotel. There was much to see.

The Rwandan government is intent on raising up the country from the ashes of the genocide. Their national parks have mountain gorillas. The poachers had their livelihoods changed as they became park rangers charged with guarding the gorillas. This created long-term ecotourism jobs. The price of seeing the mountain gorillas was $500 per person. Unfortunately, I did not capitalize on this once-in-a-lifetime opportunity to see a species what will soon be poached to extinction.

Our volunteer, Severeen, took us to an orphanage several miles from the capital. Jacque, the director of the orphanage, was in his early 40s, stocky and serious. He had hundreds of disabled wards who needed crutches, wheelchairs, prosthetics and help. He was very professional and had a shopping list for us on what was needed to help his young charges. Jacque clearly loved his people.

His shop was well organized and the tools clearly were being used on a daily basis. He was doing everything he could to improve their lot. He looked tired from working so much and yet not having the resources to do more. Without making promises we could not fulfill, we listened patiently and said we would do what we could. We were impressed and talked among ourselves about what we could do to help him out.

After the visit to Jacque' orphanage, we met with a large gathering of local leaders and what seemed like hundreds of Rwandans at a field. We stood out like a sore thumb. The young children wanted to touch my wheelchair and, not having seen white people, would touch me. They laughed and then went off and played without us.

As we traveled through the countryside on well-built, paved roads, we could see the nice clean homes that did not yet have electricity. The young Rwandans would shout out "Zumba Mazugu" which is the local slang for white person. They were smiling and waving.

Back in the capital, we met with Rwandan disabled athletes who wanted to compete in the Paralympics. They needed sports chairs and equipment. They wanted to compete internationally. But without money and sports equipment, it was not going to be possible. There were lots of single-leg amputees and a few paraplegics. One of our volunteers used braces and crutches. I have no idea how she survived the genocide. She only spoke French and was quiet.

Kigali is a beautiful modern city. Plastic bags are not allowed. Unlike other countries, there is no garbage by the side of the road. There is no graffiti. The Rwandans are very intelligent. They speak French, English and Rwandan. President Paul Kagame's plan of rebuilding Rwanda and transforming it to a First World country is working.

After dinner, we went shopping as we usually do after each distribution. This was a scouting trip. We were there to work with Rwandan organizations on the ground. We needed to set the groundwork for a wheelchair distribution and sports camp. We met with various government officials and a couple of disability organizations. Almost everything was set to go for a great distribution.

One individual had made quite the living for his family raising money in Europe. His "One Love" restaurant hotel compound was clean and had some equipment to make braces. He wanted money to make prosthetics. The equipment was dusty and Jeff and I looked at each other and smiled. Jeff and Lisa can always spot a hustle.

This man's son was in college in England. He was very well-dressed and a bit too sophisticated. With his long, braided hair, he looked like Bob Marley. He ran a restaurant, a hotel and his disability center. It did not pass the smell test. It did not look like much of his equipment was being used for anything other than fundraising.

Unlike the orphanage in the country where our Rwandan host Jacque had his hands full with disabled people and made a specific list of what he needed, this guy wanted money. Mr. One Love did not get any love.

His Bob Marley braids and small beard created an aura of charm and he was certainly personable. He talked some more about his son in London. We did not give him any money, as that is something that is just not done. Wheelchairs and crutches and maybe handcarts might be contributed to people in other countries, but no money for organizations we work with as it invites corruption.

We visited the Rwandan Genocide Memorial. When you see the pictures of children who were murdered in cold blood while the world stood by, it leaves an imprint on your mind that never leaves. It is the trauma of genocide. Those faces are watching and those sad eyes stare at you forever.

We left our hosts at the hotel and said goodbye to our charming volunteers. Our flight took us back to Brussels. At the airport Jeff and I were talking with an excited American tourist waiting for her flight. She asked us what we were doing in Rwanda. We explained that we deliver wheelchairs to disabled individuals in poor countries. She got our contact information and insisted she wanted to go on a distribution with us.

After she left for her flight, Jeff looked at me and said, "We will never see or hear from her again."

I asked him how he knew. "I've seen this all over the world. Lots of people talk. Very few people will do." He was right. We never heard from her again.

When we got back to the United States, we started making plans to do a large distribution including sports chairs. I was contacting all of my friends in the wheelchair tennis world. We had everything lined up and the wheelchairs were going to be delivered by the ever-helpful U.S. Navy to Dar El Salaam in Tanzania. The distribution was just about ready. We needed one more piece to make this distribution puzzle whole.

We needed a driver to take the wheelchairs from Tanzania to Kigali, a small trip of 750 miles. Our volunteer Severeen wanted $30,000. We told him no. Among ourselves we said HELL NO and unfortunately that was the end of that distribution. We were really disappointed as we had everything ready to go. The hard work was done. We will not be ripped off for someone's personal gain at the expense of their own disabled. We have seen the disabled used for corruption all over the world.

Rwanda's brilliant, brave leader, Paul Kagame, is still in power. Normally a country should change leaders like parents change diapers. Politicians more often than not are so full of crap their eyes are brown. In this situation, Paul Kagame is like a wise philosopher king. He remains in power because he loves his people, not because he is in love with power. His force of personality has brought this beautiful country out of poverty. Rwanda is fortunate to have him as their leader. President Kagame appears to be above corruption. He wants all of Africa to succeed. From everything we could see, the country was the exact opposite of Afghanistan and Haiti.

The Rwandan government is very well-run. There is transparency in government and almost 70 percent of Rwanda's parliament are women, more than any country on Earth. Their currency is stable. The government is executing its big plans to lift this beautiful country out of the ashes of a terrible genocide. They are succeeding.

One day, Rwanda will be the Switzerland of Africa. The surrounding countries know their money is safe if they bank there. Evil can be overcome. You just have to be brave, look evil in the eyes and confront it. It was the brave people of Rwanda that confronted the evil of mass murder, stopped it and are now working to build up their lovely country.

Rwanda is the example of what all poor countries can do to improve their lot in life. It is only with education, a commitment to excellence and a positive attitude that we succeed. This formula holds true all over the world. Rwanda was one of the poorest countries on the planet. Today it has one of the fastest-growing economies in the world.

What happened to our volunteer who wanted $30,000 to enrich himself at the expense of Rwanda's disabled poor? We don't know. When you meet people whose interest is self-interest, not group interest, exclude them from your life. Only let people in that close circle of your life that are going to bring about a positive result. We are as strong as our weakest link. Severeen was the weak link.

The Rwandans don't need us. They are an industrious, smart people. I am certain they will figure out how to help their large disabled population. Because of this volunteer's greed, we did not do a distribution to this wonderful country.

It is sometimes better not to help out. People with good intentions often cause far more harm than those motivated by greed. Rwanda's talented disabled community can form companies, build their own prosthetics, wheelchairs, crutches and other disability equipment. They clearly have the talent to do anything from banking to ecotourism to lifting an entire country out of poverty and genocide. Building wheelchairs and prosthetics is clearly within their capability.

The fact that our volunteer is greedy does not change our opinion of Rwandans. I have complete confidence in Rwanda. Having met their engineering students in Chicago at their diaspora and watched their construction workers building beautiful homes next to the hotel where we were staying, they have talent. I think Rwandans can do anything. From scientists to engineers, they are smart and are raising their country out of poverty.

One of my friends from Mexico, Raul, built a manufacturing plant to make sport and everyday wheelchairs. He ships out his excellent wheelchairs all over the world. Raul succeeded despite having polio and having to work in a country with a corrupt government. The same can be accomplished in many parts of the world if people have some peace and a little opportunity.

I would encourage everyone that can travel to visit this beautiful country that pulled itself out of poverty, war and genocide. My hope is they will build a spaceport and use their location next to the equator to launch rockets into the heavens. Sometimes we help by not helping. The world is full of Seveerens and Mr. One Loves. But it is also full of helpful volunteers, caring leaders and beautiful environments. The Chinese are there in force. America completely missed an economic opportunity. Rwanda will succeed with or without the West. They don't need us.

Chapter Eighteen
Technology Gets Better and Better

> *"By wisdom a house is built and through understanding it is established; through knowledge its rooms are filled with rare and beautiful treasures."*
>
> *Proverbs 24:3-4 NIV*

Most of us are alive because of modern medical technology. Without wheelchairs, insulin, heart surgery, gall bladder surgery, antibiotics and various other medical procedures, even simple common medicines, many of us would not be here. Americans invent, innovate and create technological solutions for humanity and on occasion to save plants and animals.

The first wheelchair supposedly might have been for King Phillip II of Spain in 1595. We really don't know. Wheelchairs became more common in the United States in the 1930s when Harry Jennings and Herbert Everest founded Everest & Jennings. They invented these heavy folding tubular steel wheelchairs. Your grandparents might have used one. As our society progressed, the number of people with disabilities who survived thanks to medical technology increased. Technology improved and as a result, wheelchairs are much better than ever. The same is true across the board in all areas of life. From televisions to cars, technology today is better.

My light metal frame wheelchair is a vast improvement over the heavy E&J steel folding chair I had back when I first lost my ability to walk. In 1977, most public buildings were not wheelchair accessible. Prior to the improvements in technology and a change in the law, life with a major walking disability was a real pain in the ass.

Today, in the United States, accessibility is the rule, not the exception. Virtually all places in public life in the United States are wheelchair-accessible. Elevators have writing in Braille and crosswalks even make noises to signal "walk," "don't walk."

Technology has improved almost all aspects of American society. Yes, life is much better today for the disabled in the United States and in the developed world. Your cell phone is also a camera, a calculator, a video recorder, a music machine, a super-search computer. "Siri, how many billionaires are there on planet Earth?" and we get an answer. "Did the Yankees win today?" We get up-to-date sport scores.

If a person is paralyzed or partially paralyzed, blind, or deaf, technology exists that will make life better. My crutches and braces enabled me to stand and walk. Before my last bout of severe nerve pain, I used to walk everywhere. Unlike most of my disabled friends, I walked for many years until the pain became so great that this part of my life ended.

All of us who are over 50 use reading glasses. A mere 218 years ago, we did not have reading glasses, electricity, automobiles, or central heating and cooling. We also did not have medicines for depression, schizophrenia, bipolar disorder, anxiety or diabetes and various other ailments.

Technological change is the constant in modern life. Soon we will have self-driving cars and trucks. What will happen next with technology and the disabled? It depends on the nature of the disability. Better technology results in less suffering and more opportunities for the disabled here and all over the world.

We were at the 2019 Sundance Film Festival and met with the Irene Taylor Brodsky's family. They were the subject of a tremendous film about deafness and the modern world. In her compelling documentary, "Moonlight Sonata, Deafness in Three Movements," Irene tells the story of her family and their son Jonas, who underwent a cochlear implant surgery. He navigates between two worlds. Irene's parents are deaf and it is amazing how technology gives young Jonas opportunities his grandparents never had.

The partially deaf like Jonas now have much better hearing aids than in any previous time in history. As our research universities and medical centers share information, in time we may be able to grow body parts in a laboratory. The damaged body parts of a person's interior ear will be replaced with either high tech hearing aids or a replacement part grown in a lab. Hearing is a special blessing for those of us who have it. Music warms the soul. It is one of life's great pleasures. Watching Jonas play Beethoven's Moonlight Sonata was a delightful experience one just does not forget.

Would I have traveled all over the world had I not become disabled with transverse myelitis? I have no idea. Would my friends have traveled the world playing wheelchair sports had they not become disabled? We can only speculate what our lives would have been. It is not relevant to today's struggles.

The reality is humans are going to become part cyborg and maybe that will be a good thing. We will suffer less and be able to do more. Now we have exoskeletons that can get people out of wheelchairs and upright. Soon the cost will go down and this technology will get paralyzed people up and walking. With the microchips and advances in new metals, these exoskeletons will vastly improve the lives of the paralyzed.

We have apps for our cell phones that enable us to see which places are wheelchair-accessible in another country. These apps tell us where accessible restaurants are located and how we get there. That is far different from my first trip to Europe in 1992. Knowing where to go and how to get there makes life much easier for someone in a wheelchair.

We now have wheelchairs that can climb stairs. They are expensive, cumbersome and awkward. These devices are in their infancy. As they improve, they will provide better access to those of us who have spinal cord damage either from disease or injury.

Christopher Reeves' motorized wheelchair was operated with his mouth. The fancy computerized talking wheelchair of Professor Stephen Hawking, both of these devices enabled them to survive. They continued to communicate and participate in society after they lost their mobility. Their lives were extended.

Hawking was an exceptional scientist and one of the smartest humans who ever lived. Technology enabled him to stay with us long after he was diagnosed with amyotrophic lateral sclerosis (ALS). He miraculously lived until 2018.

Christopher Reeves started his foundation on research to solve the riddle of how to repair spinal cord injuries. While some progress has been made in the 40 plus years I have been in a wheelchair, we have to be patient. A treatment for paralysis might or might not happen.

Nerve cells are among the most complex entities in the universe. With our vastly improved computer systems, we will be able to unravel the mysteries of what makes nerve systems work and how to repair them.

After you unwrap the covering over the spine, also known as the myelin sheath, and move the bones of the spinal column out of the way, you get a spinal cord. This amazing and complex body part has the appearance of toothpaste. In time we will be able to circumvent spinal cord damage with computer chips and micro-wiring that bypasses the injuries.

There are numerous research foundations devoted to finding treatments to paralysis, blindness, deafness, cerebral palsy, various types of cancers, diabetes and a whole host of difficulties that plague us humans.

Along with improvements in technologies, there are the inevitable scams. Stem cells are sold to desperate people as a solution to cancer, paralysis, back pain and a whole host of difficulties. Stem cell clinics promote treatments for just about everything from knee damage, back injuries, fibromyalgia to depression. Soon stem cells will be promoted as a cure for teenage pregnancy, acne and weight loss.

Stem cells do not work in treating paralysis. If stem cells worked to repair spinal cord injuries, the major insurance companies, the Social Security Administration and other governments would immediately fund these treatments.

We now have artificial hands that work where once people had very basic prosthetics. These hands are so sensitive they can pick up a wine glass or fine jewelry. In time, the hands will be so perfect that the user will be able to type as if these were their natural body parts.

Recently I was watching a young woman running with her boyfriend at a nice park in Salt Lake. She was fit and obviously worked out regularly. Her left leg was amputated above the knee near the top of her femur. Her mechanical leg was amazing. The foot adjusted to her gate. She did not miss a beat.

I have several friends who are amputees. The technology to replace amputated body parts will continue to develop. The number of amputees is going to vastly increase. As more people lose limbs to diabetes, this will be a growing market for innovative devices. Changing the diet and preventing type two diabetes is a better solution.

The costs of these replacement body parts continue to go down. With improvements in 3D printing and increased demand, replacement hands, arms and legs will soon become more available to everyone in need.

Medical technology has reached the point where people can have heart transplants. Soon artificial hearts will make their way into the market. Replacement livers, kidneys and bones are now common but expensive medical procedures.

It would be nice if we could change national law and make organ donations the rule upon death, not the exception. There is a constant shortage and long lines for people who need new kidneys and livers as well as other body parts. Changing the law where your organs are automatically donated is a better solution.

Regardless of the improvements in medical technology, the human body is a carbon-based life form with a biological clock. The cells will only divide so many times. Eventually death takes us all. Technology can go only so far in helping people improve their lives. The rest has to be done by the individual. But having a wheelchair or crutches to get around helps.

> *"Yet you do not know what tomorrow will bring. What is your life? For you are a mist that appears for a little time and then vanishes."*
>
> *James 4:14*

Chapter Nineteen

There is Hope

"Find rest, oh my soul, in God alone; my hope comes from him. He alone is my rock and my salvation; he is my fortress. I will not be shaken."

Psalm 62:5-6 NIV

When we first become disabled, we go into shock. Our entire world is turned upside down. I went from being a college athlete to crawling on the ground, desperate for a wheelchair. We had to temporarily "borrow" one from the University of Utah Medical Center. My immediate thought was, "what am I going to do now?"

That question is repeated over and over again all over the world by millions of people who are new to disability. The reality of life is we must make hard adjustments if we are going to stay alive.

We have to face our fears and start over. People with spinal cord injuries would have died in another age. But for technology, we all would be dead, spinal cord injuries or not. Throughout history, people constantly died from war, famine or disease. Death was the cure for societies' ills. Death kept the gene pool clean. Historically, there was no hope for people with major disabilities. We were feared and shunned. Our lives are now on overtime.

Animals die when they become disabled, old and are weak. But not the human animal, only humans live after they suffer a major injury or illness. It is normal for animals to be killed off by predators when they can't run fast enough or fight back. Human animals keep their elderly, their vulnerable youth and those who are disabled alive, sometimes in constant pain. But predators are still out there and hungry. Human predators will come after you.

Quit sulking and make a new life plan. Now this is easy for me to say because my dream of being an attorney and writer just meant I would do all my work sitting down. When I go to Court and the judge walks in and says, "Please be seated," I always tell the Court, "Your Honor, I brought my own chair."

It is very easy for me to tell those new to disability to do something else. "Do something besides construction work. Find a new career, you can't clean windows anymore." Advice is easy when you don't have to follow it. So is giving up.

You learn the hard way when you become disabled, regardless of how much family or friend support you have, that surviving is still up to you. Predators are waiting, including family members who will turn on you. How will you survive and be "happy"? That ridiculous word means whatever you want it to mean. There are certain behaviors I have seen work.

I met disabled people all over the world who laugh, have families, success and enjoy life. A disability is not the key to unhappiness. Even with constant physical pain, failure does not have to be an option.

What you endured to survive has made you different. You have a missing limb, a bad back, poor vision, lousy hearing, name your disability. You also have a choice. Being unhappy is a choice. You can create great memories.

The big difference now is that because you lost your mobility, you take your "bike" everywhere. From the bathroom, to the bedroom, the theater, a swimming pool, restaurant, you will be on your "bike." Your wheelchair goes with you.

One part of your life will be better. You will not be upset by minor slights, small problems and the pettiness or hateful comments of others. What would have bothered you when you were able-bodied no longer matters. You find the petty lies and crass behaviors of others ridiculous. Will you still have hope? Will you still enjoy life? Is it over? No, it is not. God still loves you.

Other than Afghanistan, Somalia, Haiti, Saudi Arabia, Yemen and numerous countries where there is no system of law, you will have hope. In Afghanistan, given the hatred of the Taliban, there is no hope. That is not your situation.

Living in the United States, Mexico, Canada or another developed nation has great advantages. Where I live in Utah, we have the National Abilities Center, (NAC). In the winter, there is a world-class ski program for people with various types of disabilities. I used to ski with them regularly when I was younger. I used to ski "pretty" and make these slow, beautiful turns. The speedsters would leave me in their snow dust. Winter does not have to be sheer hell.

What can a disabled person do in warm weather? I love to play tennis and do that on a regular basis, at least twice or three times a week in good weather. But thanks to organizations like NAC and people like Meeche White, the center's former president, summer is not drudgery. There are sports organizations for people who have disabilities all over the United States and in other countries.

My friend Dr. Myles Cope took me to Park City to NAC on a hot summer evening. Dr. Cope is physically very strong and wanted to go mountain biking. When I was able-bodied, I would go out to the West Deseret and race motorcycles. Mountain biking is very similar to racing motorcycles in the desert. There is the instant adrenalin rush from going fast on a mountain trail. Those distant memories long buried from a playful youth came back. You remember what it was like having fun on a motorcycle chasing jackrabbits and coyotes.

If you are willing to take a risk, Park City, Utah, is a beautiful mountain community with world-class skiing, mountain biking, the Sundance Film Festival and great restaurants. When you are new to disability, you have to create entirely new good memories. You are not going to do that sitting at home watching television and sulking about what you cannot do.

Go fishing. You remember going fishing when you were able-bodied. The hot sun would beat down on you. The reward of catching another living being and knowing it will soon be dinner, that feeling of success is still there. Pick your fishing spot. From lakes to streams to the ocean, in the United States, we take very good care of our marine resources. Yes, we can still go fishing.

One of my great joys is deep sea fishing off the coast of Mazatlan. We use what we catch to feed the athletes and volunteers at the World Access Project wheelchair tennis tournament.

River rafting is fun. You will have to accept help from the able-bodied community. Put your pride aside and accept physical help. You will have a great time. Grand Junction, Colorado, has excellent river rafting. So does Green River, Utah, the Rio Grande near Taos, New Mexico, and numerous other places.

Swimming is great fun and very good exercise. So is snorkeling and scuba diving. The world under the waves is full of life. There is no reason not to go swimming, snorkeling or scuba diving.

I swim at the University of Utah's terrific swimming pool. Dr. Cope likes to swim in the ocean. Snorkeling off the coast of Cancun is fun. Hawaii has nice reefs.

My friend Jesse Lee Hinson, former Paralympian, lives in Australia. He loves to go surfing. He competes in surfing competitions in Hawaii. My disabled friends in San Diego are constantly in the ocean.

You can still enjoy live music, a movie, a symphony, a lecture, a public debate, the madness of crowds. But that will not happen if you stay at home and watch others. You have to get rid of your fear of embarrassment because you are in a wheelchair and appreciate that you have been given extra time.

You will be required to be mentally stronger to survive and succeed. Success is possible and so is a great time. You will have to push yourself beyond what was your limit when you were able-bodied.

You will still enjoy Thanksgiving dinner and opening Christmas presents with loved ones. You will have friends. Life will be different. But your happiness is something you will have to work on to achieve. Being content with life is your choice.

What will happen to your personal life? If you had relationship problems when you were able-bodied, multiply them by ten when you are disabled. Divorce and breaking up is a probability unless you met *after* you became disabled. It is a very serious deal. Many partners will not be able to handle it.

You cannot have any fear of being alone. You were born alone and you die alone. It's ok to be alone. It's not a bad thing. Just accept your relationship status and move on. If you are afraid of being alone, buy a dog or a cat.

Predators will see your disability as looking at you as prey. They will go after you.

How will you be able to enjoy life when your body is broken? Well, your entire body is not broken, just parts of it. Use what works and keep what is left in absolutely great shape. This means your arms are also your legs. It also means you have to take staying in shape and your weight seriously. Eat healthy, exercise and you will survive. It is one thing to be obese when you are able-bodied. In a wheelchair, it is a disaster. Your arms cannot handle the extra weight and in time your rotator cuffs are damaged.

Many of my friends who are wheelchair athletes are in better physical shape than most able-bodied people. My friends who are in wheelchairs are not necessarily unhappy. They are not as troubled by drama, chaos or slight remarks from failed individuals who use words as arrows to hurl at others.

You survived the accident, the illness, that gunshot wound and now you are on crutches and/or a wheelchair. In any other time in history and in many parts of the world, you would be buried. Your funeral would be brief. The pain in your back and the headaches would be gone.

There is more to life than being warehoused with just a pulse and a television. But if you were a couch potato, a drunk or a drug addict before your accident or illness, that is probably what life is going to be after. Unless you completely change your mindset, you will be a loser in a wheelchair. The biggest disability in life is from the shoulders up. If you want to control that disability, control your thoughts.

To some degree, we are what we think. If we are suspicious, jealous, angry, insecure, or — worse yet —dishonest, we have to look in the mirror and ask our mortal enemy and best friend what is causing these thoughts. To succeed in sports, in business or in life we have to be cool under pressure and as unemotional as possible. Concentrate on the work and the result will take care of itself.

Be honest with yourself and your abilities. Push yourself to your limits and keep pushing a little more. Do one more lap around the park, go one more mile on that parkway next to the river, you can do it. If you have not worked up a sweat you have not worked hard enough.

Don't be afraid of a little anger. Controlled anger can help you in sports if you can maintain it and not allow it to be rage. Use your burning anger to motivate you to succeed, to push yourself harder. Uncontrolled anger will land you in jail or back in the hospital.

It's ok to feel nervous. Before a wrestling, boxing, tennis match or a big court appearance, I was always nervous. This is a good thing. It prepares you for the fight. Channel that nervousness and anger and use it to make the fight intense.

The key to enjoying life with a major disability is to stay in the moment. It is so easy to reminisce about a life you once had. Your life was supposed to end. You got some overtime.

"Therefore I tell you do not worry about your life, what you will eat or drink; or about your body, what you will wear. Is not life more important than food, and the body more important than clothes? Look at the birds of the air; they do not sow or reap or store away in barns, and yet your heavenly father feeds them. Are you not much more valuable than they?"

Matthew 6: 25-26

Where do you live? If you get a major physical disability in a small rural community, you will be challenged. There are lots of fields, stairs at the neighbors and in your own house. Your tractor does not have an elevator. Your horse does not have an accessible saddle. Your ranch life is gone. Now what?

We have to accept the reality that "overtime" does not necessarily mean we get to spend it doing what we used to do prior to our disability. You can still use your mind. Use it.

My friends work as doctors, accountants, construction managers, contractors and in many other areas of society. Other friends in wheelchairs teach school, work as youth counselors, design homes, do engineering- they do something. They have success.

Would the hundreds of people I know who have disabilities and live in many parts of the world have success had they not become disabled? Are they over-achievers? I think they did what they had to do to succeed by taking the risk of education and overcoming their fears. They are not their disability. Our wheelchair is not who we are, only how we get to where we are going. You walk, we roll.

With a strong belief in God, the hope for a better tomorrow is always there. The reason we should have hope is we survived. Why did we survive? If we believe in God, as we do, we see the world differently. I believe we survived for a reason or for many reasons. Serve God and we will be just fine.

"Each one should use whatever gift he has received to serve others, faithfully administering God's grace in its various forms."

1 Peter 4:10

Chapter Twenty

Serving the Lord Is a Gift

"My heart is changed within me; all my compassion is aroused."

Hosea 11:8[b] NIV

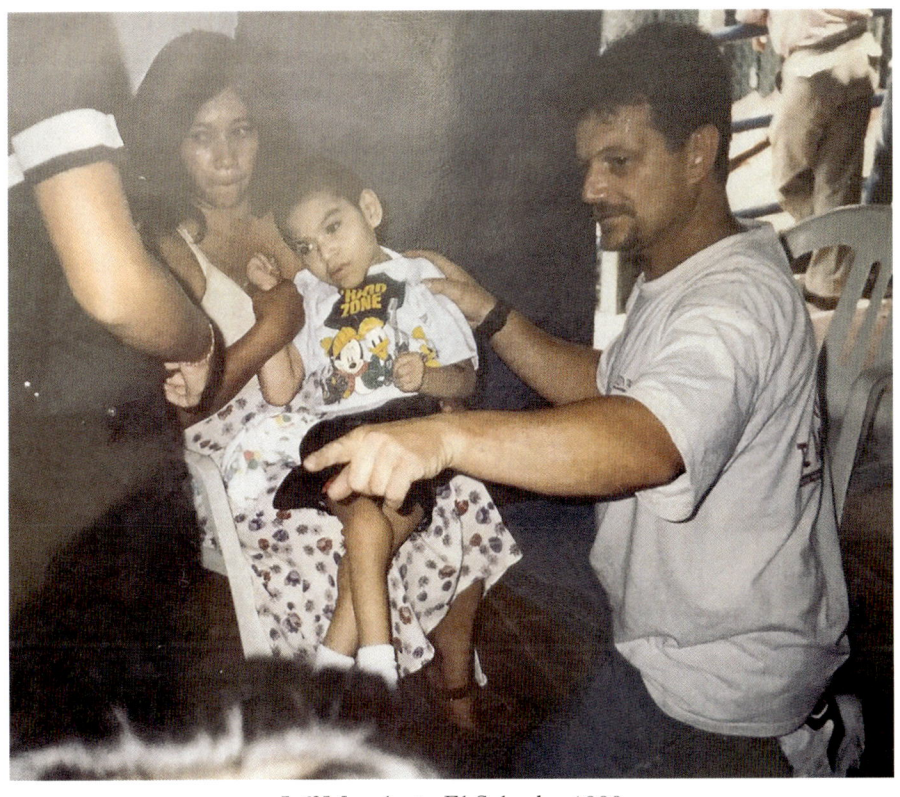

Jeff Murphy in El Salvador 1999

    Letting the Mobility Project go was one of the most difficult things I ever experienced. We were heartbroken. The financial situation nationwide changed for everyone. Our donors' financial support was a gift, not a mandatory expense. It was not an obligation. We understood that. We were cruising along, trying to bring in enough money to keep us up and running from month to month. It was good. We sent out quarterly letters and communicated with donors and volunteers. This was our life. The life God prepared in advance for us to do.

Three months after the financial crash, we had to make a decision. It was like losing my best friend. I felt the Mobility Project was my identity. It was who I was: Lisa, the president of the Mobility Project. This was painful. People were supportive. Some of our partners begged us to continue. We were all hoping the recession might be a glitch, a short stint in our country's financial institutions.

I think all Americans wanted to be hopeful. We hoped from month to month that we could catch up. But as time went on and the recession got worse, it was inevitable that we could not. For the two years I was able to pull a salary, I put almost all of it right back in to keeping the Mobility Project alive.

All other staff would raise their own support as we did at first to continue working and paying our own bills. This takes an extreme amount of work and causes financial stress like we had never faced before. Asking for money for the disabled poor in other countries is one of the most difficult tasks I had ever done. The faces of the men, women and children we were able to lift up off the ground all over the world kept us focused on the prize. It was all for them, the disabled, not for us. Some people do not understand the concept of giving. The humanitarian work brought great joy to our lives. Even our own families had a hard time with our work. This was difficult.

Finally, we met with our board of directors. We made the decision to shut down the Mobility Project. I was no longer receiving paychecks and could not pay the bills at the home office. We knew we could not last forever. It was not just my decision. This was one of the most difficult decisions of our lives. It had become our baby. I felt like I would be nothing without this work. This was my life and I loved it.

As I look back, I can see now how crazy this all seems. I had to get over myself, because I was not "the Mobility Project". God was "the Mobility Project" and the work we were doing. God was always the center of our work and always will be. As is said in Scripture:

> *".......let us not live with words or tongue but with actions and in truth. This then is how we know that we belong to the truth, and how we set our hearts at rest in his presence, whenever our hearts condemn us. For God is greater than our hearts, and He knows everything"*
>
> *1 John 3:18-20*

With time, life moved on. The pain of this loss got easier. I almost felt guilty as the financial pressure from this work lessened. As the months went on and the wound from this loss healed, I realized this time in our lives was over. We had to trust God and the reality that the door had closed and a new path was ahead.

The good that came from the Mobility Project far outweighed the sadness of this loss in helping others. The organizations that now exist because of the Mobility Project are amazing. It was time for others to carry the torch. We could still volunteer with others and contribute on another level. This was very different but still exciting. If I stopped serving God, this would be my choice, not His. He does not stop working in us as long as we seek Him with a pure heart.

"Look to the Lord and his strength, seek his face always."

Psalm 105:4

The Mobility Project worked because of our tremendous volunteers. The passion was infectious. People really understood that to serve with us was not difficult. No special skills were needed, just a good heart. When you came into the field with us, you were needed. All of you. There was this feeling of satisfaction and meaning like no other.

Some people who had no relationship with God became believers because volunteers said they could see a love and bright light in our service like no other. Our gratitude for them is so great and serving alongside them created some of the best memories in our entire life! Here are some of their stories.

Jeff Murphy
Director, Mobility Project
Las Vegas, Nevada

In my 30s after we moved, I made a drastic career change into medical equipment, meaning mostly wheelchairs. I realized how important mobility is for so many people, especially people without insurance. This is when I started saving/collecting useful equipment that was being tossed by nursing homes, etc. I really didn't know what I was going to do with it, but I knew I could help people when they needed a small part or even a whole wheelchair for a short time.

When Lisa and I were in Mexico on a pretty perfect vacation, we saw people crawling on the ground with no wheelchairs in sight. Lisa and I tried to find wheelchairs for purchase and could not find even one. I knew then that God had put this desire in my heart.

After hooking up with the Mobility Project, we delivered wheelchairs all over the world. All my equipment was refurbished and shipped out to countries that were in need.

On our first trip to Nicaragua, we repaired many wheelchairs. I was actually amazed that I knew exactly how to fix every chair with the parts provided. I even knew to ask if people had wounds. A man came in with a stage 4 wound on his right leg. I was able to help him as I read the book "Where There Is No Doctor." I even had the book on me to reference. I learned how to pack wounds with honey and other practical things.

At the end of the day, I still wondered what my gift was when Lisa turned to me and said, "This is your gift". I mention this because so many people wonder what their gift is and it is usually what you enjoy doing the most. It's something that is — a part of you and has always been a strong suit. We just can't see it in ourselves. I had no idea that for the next 14 years or so we would travel to just about every poor country that I would never have wanted to visit. It was an honor to be able to serve in this way. You learn a lot about people when you visit poor countries.

It was such a blessing to be able to work with such amazing people all over the world. It was more than I could have ever dreamed my life would be. When it's a "gift," it's a pleasure to serve.

One of the most profound moments was in El Salvador. We were seating children. A woman came in carrying her son and I noticed she was limping. We took care of her son and when she got up to leave, I noticed that her ankle was broken. The bone was actually sticking out and it had scabbed over. This was a very old injury. We asked her about it and she said she could not afford medical care. Right there and then between all the volunteers we raised about $600 to take care of it.

She was in a hurry as she was dressed in a work uniform and was on her way to work. Can you just imagine the pain this woman was in? We paid for a cab for her also so she would not have to walk to the bus. I thought this is a mother's love for her child displayed like I have never seen before.

She was very grateful. There were tears all around. She never asked for anything and was quite content with just a wheelchair for her son. She left with so much hope but left me so much more. As we always said, these memories were our paydays, but also so much more ....

I will always remember the people in small villages such as Jinotepe in Nicaragua, Parwan in Afghanistan and Quetta in Pakistan. Their eyes would well up with tears when we were leaving. They would express to us that they would always remember us on that day in the future as "The day the wheelchair people came and changed our lives." It will be a "celebrated holiday," they would tell us. I was so humbled and thankful to be used by God in this way.

Pastor Peter Voorhees
Calvary Chapel
Silverdale, Washington

I didn't know much about The Mobility Project on my first trip in 2000. I was interning at a bible college in Austria. Part of my requirements as an intern was to lead a trip of students on short-term mission trip somewhere in Europe. Jeff and Lisa let me know they were headed to Pakistan with the Mobility Project to minister to a few hundred people. They had a list of people in need of wheelchairs.

The people that were seated in chairs during our time there varied in their specific needs. There were children who lost their legs because they had stumbled upon landmines still buried from previous wars. Men and women were amputees due to infection had lost a limb. A number of people affected with polio. There were various deformities that didn't allow them to be as mobile as they could be. It was life-changing to be there and a part of truly a life-giving, humanitarian, Jesus-filled, no-way-they-could-pay-us-back, love-filled, cross-cultural experience.

There are so many good memories. There were five of us: Daniel, Ken, Greg, Kevin, and me. Daniel and Kevin were able to look and blend in some degree with the Pakistani people. Greg, Ken and I are all above six feet, Caucasian, and as different looking from the Pakistanis as possible. Greg has fiery red hair, Ken is a platinum blond, and I couldn't grow facial hair if my life depended on it. The Pakistanis tend to be an average of five feet to five feet six inches tall, have dark skin, facial hair and black hair more often than not.

As Christians, we were a little concerned by some of the stories that we had heard coming out of Pakistan. This is a Muslim country. The leadership of the school in Austria initially did not allow us to go. The concern was for our safety while in country. After a few conversations and much prayer, we were given the green light to proceed with the trip.

We had to deliver the wheelchairs to the village where we would be seating individuals the next day. We all piled into the truck and headed out of the city to the town 45 minutes away. There was a possibility of checkpoints by the military that might cause some trouble.

We had on traditional Pakistani dress and tried to look as inconspicuous as possible. I do remember that we were stopped at one checkpoint and everyone was really nervous. I was told to take off my eyeglasses as they gave me away as a foreigner. I couldn't see anything. After sitting in the truck while our driver spoke with the military personnel, we were eventually on our way again. After we got moving again, I put my glasses back on.

I didn't see what happened in the interchange. I was praying throughout the foreign conversation that was taking place. It was a moment of faith for me. With my glasses on, I was able to have some understanding of our surroundings. I could see. I could make out what was around us. We were in potential danger by virtue of just being us. It was where we're from, what we believe, and our perceived value to someone that might want to exploit us for their gain.

When I took off my glasses and heard a conversation I couldn't understand, there was a deep sense of helplessness. In prayer, there was a real dependence on God to order what would happen next. I was at the mercy of those around me. As we passed through the checkpoint, my heart was racing. It was a time that has stuck with me to this day.

There are times where I won't be able to see or understand what is going on around me. Sometimes I'm going to have to rely on others to see me through a difficulty. In all circumstances, the Lord will direct my footsteps and bring me through whatever trial I find myself.

"We walk by faith and not by sight when we follow Jesus Christ as our Lord and Savior."

2 Corinthians 5:7, Hebrews 11:6

On the way back, I would ride in the bed of the truck with our armed escort. Everywhere we went in Pakistan, we had an armed escort. Not the most trained crack squad of individuals, but the organization that the Mobility Project teamed up with felt we needed them.

In the back of the truck, the guard and I struck up a conversation. He spoke English. I've always wanted to learn phrases from native speakers in how to say certain things: "What's your name?" "Hello!" "Goodbye!" "Where's the bathroom?" ... All the important stuff. As our guard and I were in the back of the truck, his automatic rifle strapped to his chest, I asked him what he does for a living.

"So are you security full-time or do you work another job?" He responded, saying he teaches The Koran. (Gulp)... so what happens when you ask someone a question about what they do ... they ask you, "What do you do?" Again, one of those ... Do I tell him I'm a Bible teacher? Yes, I do. Again, it was my faith that this may get me in trouble. We had a great conversation about our jobs and what brings us joy.

We would go out to the demilitarized zone to minister to a community of people in the northern part of the country. There was a HUGE sign that implied, "You're on your own past this point." It wasn't quite that blunt, but it was close.

We pulled into the ancient citadel, adobe walls and compound. We would meet the chief of the tribe and see the individuals we would be seating. The women on one side and men on the other.

The men of the tribe would have to give their women permission to be seen by us in order for us to seat them. I was moved by the sense of ancient hospitality that they showed us. While we were with them, they protected us as if we were one of their own. They were really grateful for what we provided and the care, respect and love that was shown.

We met a Christian missionary there named John. He was there with his 2-year-old boy. John was sharing with us what the ministry looked like there in Pakistan. It was a ministry of prayer. It was not a ministry where there was a lot of resources. The Pakistani government had a state sponsored/backed Christian church that they allowed. That didn't mean the people accepted it, but they didn't have to fear government persecution.

John taught me about prayer in a very powerful way. There were about 10 of us in the room talking with him. A few were carrying on the conversation when John's son started fussing and crying. His son was obviously uncomfortable. Daniel and I looked at John as his son was fussy.

John placed his hands on his son's belly, closed his eyes, and slightly bowed his head. In less than 15 seconds, John's baby was still and content. John then opened his eyes and continued to participate in the conversation. Daniel and I looked at each other and mouthed something like, "Did you just see that?" We were both ministered to by John's demonstration of prayer and creating peace for his son through prayer. It was powerful.

All of us got some sort of Pakistani bug or virus. I won't go into detail as to the different things our bodies did, but it wasn't good. After coming back from Pakistan, I think it took all of us a week or two to get back to normal. Pakistan is a smelly country. The sewers are open and running along the street. When we were met by classmates at the airport upon returning, we had to roll down the windows because our clothes smelled so bad.

It was a memorable trip for so many reasons. We learned about ourselves, the people we came into contact with, our team, and how God wants to use us if we are available to change lives for the better.

Pakistan was my first trip with the Mobility Project. I would then accompany them on other trips leading groups of people to Mexico and El Salvador. So many stories, so many lives changed, and so many life lessons learned. I'm grateful for the time I was able to participate in seating people in wheelchairs with the Mobility Project.

Jeff and Lisa Murphy are the reason I had such a life-changing experience. Chip Matthingly, Steve Oliver, Ray Terrill, Alex Rice, and others have always been great to connect with. It was Jeff and Lisa that made the Mobility Project what it was. They are the ones that made it so effective and helped so many people. I've been struck recently by the reality of Jesus' words regarding the sheep and goats in Matthew 25.

> *"When the Son of Man comes in his glory, and all the angels with him, then he will sit on his glorious throne. Before him will be gathered all the nations, and he will separate people one from another as a shepherd separates the sheep from the goats. And he will place the sheep on his right, but the goats on the left. Then*

the King will say to those on his right, 'Come, you who are blessed by my Father, inherit the kingdom prepared for you from the foundation of the world. For I was hungry and you gave me food, I was thirsty and you gave me drink, I was a stranger and you welcomed me, I was naked and you clothed me, I was sick and you visited me, I was in prison and you came to me.' Then the righteous will answer him, saying, 'Lord, when did we see you hungry and feed you, or thirsty and give you drink? And when did we see you a stranger and welcome you, or naked and clothe you? And when did we see you sick or in prison and visit you?' And the King will answer them, 'Truly, I say to you, as you did it to one of the least of these my brothers, you did it to me.'

"Then he will say to those on his left, 'Depart from me, you cursed, into the eternal fire prepared for the devil and his angels. For I was hungry and you gave me no food, I was thirsty and you gave me no drink, I was a stranger and you did not welcome me, naked and you did not clothe me, sick and in prison and you did not visit me.' Then they also will answer, saying, 'Lord, when did we see you hungry or thirsty or a stranger or naked or sick or in prison, and did not minister to you?' Then he will answer them, saying, 'Truly, I say to you, as you did not do it to one of the least of these, you did not do it to me.' And these will go away into eternal punishment, but the righteous into eternal life."

Matthew 25:31-46

Jesus says that those who are his, the sheep, are the ones who feed the hungry, who give the thirsty a drink, welcoming the stranger, clothing the naked, visiting the sick, coming to those in prison, and I would imagine it would fit as well … giving the gift of mobility through a wheelchair to those who can't walk. The Mobility Project was a ministry that fulfilled the great commandment of loving God and loving people. We can't truly love God unless we love people. We love people because that's what God demonstrates to us… he loves us with a love we could never repay.

None of these families could ever afford to repay or do anything in return to "earn" these wheelchairs, but they are given because they have value as human beings. Man, woman, child, Buddhist, Muslim,

Christian, Atheist, Agnostic, Mexican, Pakistani, American, African ... they all have worth because they are created in the image of God. The Mobility Project validated their worth and dignity by giving them the gift of mobility without condition. I'm grateful for the time I was able to help contribute to the effort.

Michiel Shaw
Director, Mobility Project
Silverdale, Washington
Costa Rica

Although it's been quite some time since my last opportunity to travel with The Mobility Project, the experience remains vivid in my heart and mind. We arrived at our wheelchair distribution site in Costa Rica at what we thought was an early hour, only to find dozens of people already waiting for us. My first thought was how humbling it was to see their excited faces. The complete acceptance of having to wait, no matter how long, to have a chance for their loved one to receive a wheelchair. The recipients would all be children.

We started unpacking the wheelchairs we had shipped, and setting up our "seating" area. I came to understand that I was expected to help fit the chairs to the people. The fact that I didn't know one end of a screwdriver from another and possessed no technical skills did not seem to matter to my fellow workers. With great patience they taught me how to do the simplest jobs, and I managed to feel marginally useful.

People kept coming all day, every day we were there. Some from many miles away, often carrying their children the entire way. Some of the children were older, but had virtually never been outside their home because there was simply no way to transport them. No school. No parties. No "normal." We kept very busy, energized by the smiles of amazement on the kids' faces, and the tears of gratitude from their families.

Until joining the Mobility Project, I had never given much thought to the wheelchair needs of people in other countries. During an earlier trip to Bulgaria, I was part of a small group that, among other tasks, delivered two wheelchairs to the biggest hospital in the capital Sofia. We discovered they previously had only one wheelchair in the entire facility.

I began to understand that this was a great need in many places. When Jeff and Lisa Murphy started the Mobility Project, they recognized the prison these kids lived in and set out to do what they could. God put on their hearts the desire and will, and provided the means for many years. My ignorance of these needs was gloriously eliminated as I had the privilege to work with them, and with these beautiful families in Costa Rica and other countries. I can honestly say I received far more than I ever gave.

Alex Rice
Administrator, Mobility Project
Colorado Springs, Colorado

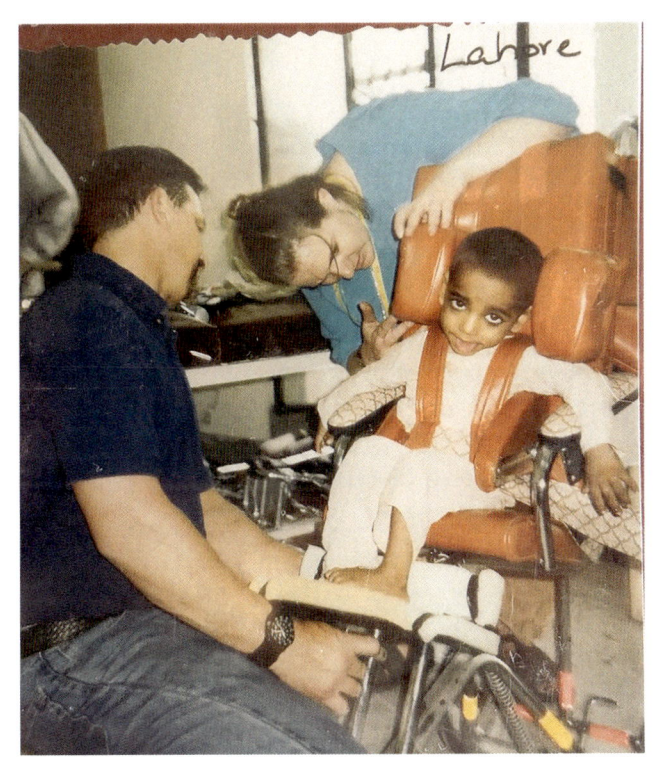

Jeff Murphy and Alex Rice

When I was 17 years old, I had my life all planned out. Call it wishful thinking or teenage naivety, but consequently my life has not turned out in any way that I had planned. The first event of the demise of my plans was saying "yes" to an innocent invitation to join a new team being formed to deliver some wheelchairs. Stepping onto the plane that day, I had no idea how my life would be changed. I would be ruined for the ordinary. The next 11 years of my life would be filled with numerous trips around the world, each one fueling an addiction to finding transformation.

In the crowds at a distribution, we often would see the most desolate parts of humanity. Hopelessness filled the eyes of so many and looking out into the waiting areas is where most of my memories lie. I remember one woman in a small town in El Salvador. She was elderly, very frail and sickly looking. Her skin was pale, and her eyes clouded over in a mindless haze. Her son had left her on a folding lawn lounger where she stayed all day waiting her turn. He came back from work periodically to check on her and see if her number had been called. I was concerned for her and walked by often to touch her arm and make sure she was still breathing!

Later that day, Lisa realized that the next number at our administration table was 5000. This meant that the next person being fit would be the 5,000th person to receive a wheelchair from the Mobility Project. This called for a celebration. I ran to all three stations telling them that the race was on for the 5,000th "customer".

At the third station was the woman in the lawn chair and I barely recognized her. I was astonished as she looked like a totally different person! Just sitting up and having the attention of a small group of people who were interacting with her was stimulation that she probably hadn't had in a very long time. Seating her in her new chair was Steve Oliver, then president of the Mobility Project. He had decided at the last minute to jump in to seat someone.

As the race began, our whole team began cheering for each station to finish. Our excitement spread to the crowd when they caught on to the significance of this race. Steve and the "lawn chair lady" finished seconds before another station. She had a giant smile on her face as the excitement surrounded her. Steve still had to get her to the registration area for the picture. A literal race took place between two old ladies being pushed in wheelchairs for the first time racing down a hallway.

We all were laughing so hard and cheering when Steve and this sweet lady won the race. Better than being the 5,000th recipient of a wheelchair, was the transformation that took place with this woman in just a short hour. She looked years younger, her complexion was a normal color, and the death that had covered her had now been lifted and replaced with life. The clouded look lifted from her eyes and I could see brilliant blue shine through. A beautiful smile spread across her face. The best sound came from her lips, the laughter of someone who has not laughed nearly enough in her life.

Another time in western Pakistan, a man came into our distribution, clearly having walked a very long distance. He carried a cloth bundle over his shoulder. When he arrived, he put the bundle down on the ground. Out rolled two balls of what I originally thought were clothes. In disbelief I saw that these balls were actually two girls with a form of both dwarfism and scoliosis which made it easy for them to roll into a small ball.

When it was their turn to receive a wheelchair, they literally rolled into the room tucking their useless, deformed legs under their chin and propelling themselves forward with their arms. I carefully unfolded each one to reveal twin teenage girls with the most brilliant green eyes I have ever seen. I smiled a "hello" at them. Then I spent the hour getting to know them. I was seating them in their new wheelchairs and watching them blossom into confident young women. They may have rolled into my station eye level with the ground, yet they wheeled out with dignity and a new-found hope for the future.

Sometimes the transformation could be a little harder to see. I have met so many young men with cerebral palsy in my travels. This disease imprisons the person in their body as their mind is clear. But, their body just won't cooperate. Their muscles become hard and rigid often racked with spasms. Speaking can be difficult as well as mobility and each person has a unique battle. But even when it was hard to communicate, I could look into their eyes and be able to see who they were deep inside, past the disability. The before and after of their eyes was always there to see, if you were looking for it.

But the most captivating transformation was from the women of Afghanistan covered under the veil of a burqa. The mesh netting would not let me see their eyes and were designed to make them invisible to the outside world. These women were so demoralized having survived the tyranny of the Taliban and the oppression of their culture. They were not allowed to speak. Their faces were required to be covered, just for being a woman. The women who were lucky enough to be allowed to have a wheelchair would be fitted in my station.

Sometimes I would hear a barely audible whisper of a "Thank you" in Dari or Pashto. When no one was looking, some women would grab my hand for a quick squeeze of thanks. Sometimes there was only me looking into their burqa and swearing I could *feel* a smile coming from underneath. These subtle acts of gratitude from these women impacted my life deeper than I realized at the time.

Fast forward to the present day, I have the privilege to run an organization for Afghan refugees in Colorado. Due to so many long years of war, drought, famine, and political unrest, Afghans were the largest displaced people in the world. Now, Syria's civil war has made them the largest refugee population in the world. Now I get to see past the burqa at the faces of these precious women every day in my own city!

Twenty-three years after my first trip with the Mobility Project, the journey has been long and hard. But, oh so worth it. As I look back at the plans I had for myself, I can honestly say that the plans God had for me instead were so much better. So, as you are reading this book and if you are wondering what is next in your life, I hope that you are encouraged to say "yes" and to take that first step. All of us you are reading about are just everyday ordinary people who said "yes" to God's calling. Our lives were made better for it. God uses ordinary people to do extraordinary things. Take the step. You won't regret it.

Brandon Brooks
Volunteer
Silverdale, WA

I was 14 years old when I went on my first mission trip to Mazatlan, Mexico. I had no idea that at the time the work I would be exposed to would find its way back into my life in a significant way years later.

The plan for the trip was simple: To serve the community and show them the love of Christ in practical ways. Our group of 20 or so teenagers and leaders tore down a massive concrete wall for a church and put on a vacation bible school camp for the local children. These were meaningful tasks. What had the greatest impact for me was the wheelchair outreach program we held near the end of the trip.

At that time, I had no knowledge of wheelchairs. All I had was an eager heart to serve a community that was in great need. That moment was impactful for me and would ultimately find its way back into my life years later as I became an ATP (Assistive Technology Professional) and manufacturer's representative for the largest complex rehab company in the world. I have learned that God has a way of bringing us back to experiences He used to shape us.

At the wheelchair clinic, I remember seeing a young disabled boy. I assume his diagnosis was cerebral palsy. He came in with no means of transporting himself. His family carried him from place to place. It was a very difficult task for his loved ones. Jeff Murphy and my father, Joe, worked together to fit him in his own wheelchair. I will never forget his smile and the tears on his mother's face when his very own chair was finally finished.

These are the moments that last. I consider myself blessed to have fallen into such work. I have moments like these on a weekly basis at the wheelchair clinics at Seattle Children's Hospital and Harbor View Medical Center. God used the Mobility Project in a powerful way in my life. I am grateful for the work of Jeff and Lisa Murphy and how they have impacted so many lives across the globe.

Aaron Murphy
Volunteer
Las Vegas, Nevada

The Turning Point

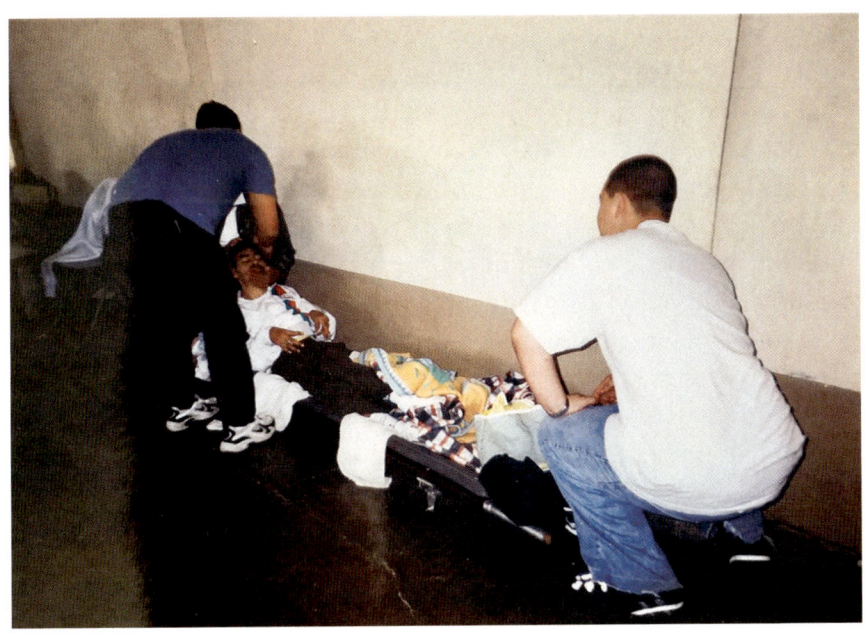

Aaron Murphy and Jeff Murphy assessing Enriqui for his new wheelchair in Guatemalla.

At this point in my life I was a typical self-absorbed teenager, more concerned about hanging out with my friends and doing what I wanted to do whenever I wanted to do it. My parents had been involved in wheelchair distributions for about a year or more. I had grown to resent the whole establishment that was the Mobility Project. I was too self-absorbed to understand the reasoning and drive as to why they even did it. All I knew is that it took time and attention away from me and, most importantly, what I wanted to do.

They had wanted to bring my siblings and me on these trips with them. I never had any motivation to go. I was the last hold-out after my brother and sister had gone on a trip to Central America. I still had no desire to go even when my ticket was already purchased by a very giving donor that knew me well. After a very eloquent speech from my mother, I finally decided to go, even though I absolutely despised every bit of the idea.

The trip was to Chimaltenango, Guatemala. This isn't a location you would generally dream of going to as a teenager. However, all of this led to a major turning point in my life. This trip has had a profound impact on the man that I am today, and the man I intend to become. I had no idea what I was getting into. But, when we got there, I was fully content either staying in the room, or shooting the basketball in the gym at the campus where we were staying. As the distribution that was planned for this trip began, I didn't know what to expect. I chose to play basketball and watch, instead of becoming involved.

One thing I would like to give my parents credit for is they never forced me to do anything. They just wanted me to be there and draw my own conclusions from the experience. As I have learned in dealings with children, this can be an amazing approach. You may not see the results for a long time, but it does work.

That is when it happened. I remember it like it was yesterday. A woman came in with her 30-year-old son, being carried on a stretcher. Some volunteers were helping her get him into position in the gym. This is where my dad would fit him for the first wheelchair of his life. I watched all of this happen while I was periodically sitting in a wheelchair and getting up every now and again to shoot the basketball. I was doing absolutely nothing to help.

My mother, whether it was intentional or not, gave me a bit of a nudge in the right direction by telling me the story about how the mother and her son came about being there. She had single handedly dragged this man on the stretcher for some 8-10 hours, while changing multiple buses to get them there in the hopes that her son could have his first real chance at mobility in 30 years. This was his first shot to have some degree of freedom.

I reflected on the information my mother gave for a few minutes before I started doing some deep soul searching. I felt a lot of emotions as I was realizing how disgustingly selfish I had been, not only in that moment but my entire life. The sitting watching and avoiding work was just a microcosm for how I had lived my life.

I felt an emotion that I can honestly say I never really felt before. I felt compassion for the man and his mother equally. They had both worked so hard and gotten through so much in their lifetimes. They kept meeting these challenges and getting through them for so long. What had I done until that point? What could I view as a challenge in my life? How truly ungrateful for what I have been given this entire time? I felt compelled to help however I could. It was an awakening.

I was unsure how I could help. I figured a good place to start would be to ask my dad. He instantly put me to work assisting him. Like a surgeon in an operating room, he was efficiently resolving complicated seating and mobility issues, as he had plenty of other people to see that day. He had me handing him tools, switching out wheelchairs, cutting foam, everything that I couldn't possibly mess up.

Getting the seating and positioning right in this situation was difficult. The general inactivity had taken a toll on the man's flexibility. Watching my dad diagnose and address his needs in such a timely manner gave me a whole different level of appreciation for his abilities.

One of the most vivid memories of my lifetime will always be when we first got him up in the chair. That man's smile could light up the room. His mother's smile was even more infectious. I couldn't even imagine the emotions streaming through their bodies in that moment, but I knew I couldn't control mine. It wasn't only life changing for them, it was life changing for me as well. I was struggling to hold back tears thinking of how happy I was for them. Even in the process of writing this, it stirs the exact same emotions that I had that day, pure joy and happiness for them.

I had no idea how long this moment would affect me. It took years for it to really take a hold on my life. I felt guilty for years after this, constantly thinking about how self-serving I had been my entire life. I still had moments after this where I had to wrestle with the same self-derived thoughts and actions.

It took quite some time before I realized through a series of maturing, reading, learning and thought, that this was a tool that has helped shape me into who I am now, and ultimately who I desire to become. It was a singular point in time that changed my way of thinking like no other moment in my life. This is a time I reflect upon frequently to keep me grounded, grateful, balanced, happy, humble, etc.…It would take me many more years after to fully realize that my parents were doing this for something that is bigger than me or them, and my relationship with them. The feeling of joy, and self-fulfillment that giving your time and effort to those that are truly in need is beyond almost any other glory in life.

Without this moment, I wouldn't have a fraction of the integrity, character and kindness that I have today. I will always be eternally grateful to my parents for introducing these principles and lifelong lessons. I will continue to try to implement these practices into every aspect of my life. Deep down in my heart I know it is the right thing to do.

Pastor Dave Grisanti
Ministry Training International
Poulsbo, Washington

My friendship and association with Jeff and Lisa Murphy goes back to around 1994. I was serving as the pastor of the church they began attending. We quickly became friends. Our daughters were close friends in junior high school at the time.

In the mid- to late 1990s I went to Bulgaria to work with a couple of churches in the capital city of Sofia. A group of three others joined me, Jeff being one of them. We each brought a wheelchair. We donated them to a large hospital in Sofia. The hospital director was very thankful. He then gave us a tour of the hospital. I saw then that a ministry of providing mobility was filling a great need.

It was around that time that I attended a conference of pastors in California. During a portion given to missions, Steve Oliver got up and spoke of his ministry of providing wheelchairs in other countries. I took his information and gave it to Jeff and Lisa. They eventually connected with him and became a part of the Mobility Project.

In 2006, I was able to finally go with them on a ministry trip, to Costa Rica. We spent a week seating people as we distributed chairs and mobility equipment. We were busy every day. I was so impressed at how well the whole project was organized and run by Lisa. She was awesome, unruffled by anything unexpected. It was an amazing time and I was privileged to be a part of that team.

Not long after that, the Mobility Project was solely in the hands of Jeff and Lisa. They continued to work joyfully and tirelessly, dedicating themselves to providing mobility worldwide. They were making the sacrifices necessary in order for it to work. I don't know how they did it all, but God always provided for their needs and the needs of the ministry.

I am glad for their enduring friendship through the years and grateful for their inspiring service to the Lord and to those in need. As you can see, the work was infectious to everyone involved.

Brock Moller
Vice president, Mobility Project
Bremerton, Washington

The Mobility Project was officially a humanitarian organization. In reality, we strove to spread the gospel in all that we did and to love people in the name of Jesus. We strove to be doves and sharp as serpents. If calling ourselves a "humanitarian organization" got us into non-Christian countries that would have otherwise banned us — and did at times — so be it. We did what we had to do to help people in need.

We frequented Mexico. Steve Oliver, now deceased, lived there. Mexico, our southern neighbor, was an easy trip just being next door. We did a lot of work in and around Mazatlan and other cities. Mazatlan was one of our highlight trips. We held a sports camp for people with disabilities. Danny Quintana, Richard St Denis and Tito Bautista are wheelchair athletes. They would show the local disabled individuals how to play wheelchair sports. We had a fantastic time. I got to witness the change in many people who believed their lives were over because of their spinal cord injury or being new to disability. Their lives were transformed, they blossomed and became advocates for an active lifestyle.

Sometimes tragedy would strike. On one of our trips in 2007, Lisa Murphy left me in charge of a sports camp. We had lunch and one of the locals that I was chatting with had a heart attack. I heard voices calling my name. I ran down to the court where they were all gathering. He had fallen out of his wheelchair. We called 911 and I tried to provide life support. He was probably dead before he hit the ground. This was a very sober moment. It reminded everyone of the importance and fleeting nature of life.

Lisa and Jeff are quite a team. Jeff is one of the best wheelchair fitters you will ever find. His expertise was essential to the humanitarian work we were doing. Jeff and Lisa gave selflessly of their time and money and used their resources to keep our small organization going.

The memories are endless. Some are quite colorful. In Afghanistan, their fledgling free-market economy had buyers and sellers of anything that could sell. They would buy and sell gasoline on the side of the road. I did not realize how little they truly had.

In Thailand, the people were wonderful. Some lived in very poor conditions. The Thai hospitality, laughter, their joy and our memories of me driving a tuk tuk in Bangkok. And there were the times of getting sick in El Salvador where one of our volunteers needed an I.V. Other warm moments of being in Costa Rica ziplining with the monkeys after we had been seating people in wheelchairs and seeing the joy it brought to their lives. Their gratitude is etched in my heart. One poor individual gave me a cheap gold watch. I still have it. He was so grateful he gave me what was most likely his most valuable possession. I had no choice but to graciously accept his gift.

One grandmother in El Salvador came up with her grandchild on her back. I think this was normal life for them. The child she was carrying was not small. How she did it, I don't know. I can only think of a statute that is in Boy's Town in Omaha, Nebraska, where I grew up. It famously says, "He's not heavy, Father, he's my brother." Well, her grandchild apparently wasn't heavy either. I will say, the tears that streamed from all of our eyes when they left — he in a wheelchair and her pushing — made me want to do such things all the time.... So I did.

Going back to Afghanistan, we were outside of Kabul at a hospital. Brad Moore and Havala Holmes were sick. We were seating people in wheelchairs. A man dragged himself to the distribution on custom-fit "gloves" he had made out of a pieces of car tires. He dragged himself around in this manner with his tire gloves on his hands and knees to protect them from the ground. He was a paraplegic. Like so many other paraplegics we met, he had no use of his lower extremities. The source of his condition was war with the Russians. Needless to say, he left there with his tire pieces on his lap as he rolled away in his new wheelchair.

One memory burns in my heart. That is the long lines of people waiting for wheelchairs everywhere we went. I remember the loving work of NGOs finding the people who needed mobility, spreading the word far and wide in local communities. People are people, and therefore imperfect. There was selfishness, theft as some would come back for a second chair so they could sell the first. We weren't there to judge. But, we did our best to be prudent and good stewards of what we were giving away.

There were rough times. The work was not "comfortable." Not that the locals didn't try their best to provide for us, which they most certainly did. But resources were scarce and we had a job to do. In many of the places we went, often it was hot. Air conditioning was minimal to non-existent. We were there for them. At the end of the day, our comfort wasn't the goal. Safety was important.

There were times, such as when the Taliban was still in charge in Afghanistan, that even extreme safety measures weren't all that safe. The important thing is, as we used to say, the safest place to be is where God has you. All of us on some level felt called to be right where we were.

I love the people of Afghanistan. Alex Rice has a ministry in Colorado serving people in the U.S. from Afghanistan. I love the people of Mexico. Richard St Denis lives in Mexico, ministering there. I love the people of Costa Rica, Thailand, El Salvador and all of the places the Mobility Project delivered wheelchairs.

Unfortunately, I did not go to every country where the Mobility Project delivered wheelchairs, countries in Africa, South America, Pakistan, Vietnam just to name a few. I can give you my testimonial that this is a wonderful world filled with many different people, cultures and many perspectives.

The Mobility Project changed my life. The perspective I gained traveling around this big blue planet, I am excited to help my boys who were not yet born when I was doing this work. This will help them gain perspective and truth.

The real protagonist of this story is God. The Antagonist is Satan, the devil, evil, bad — however you look at the opposite of good. The players, many of whom I've spoken of and others I have thought about, Dutch Meyer, Hans & Dorothy Ariens, Karen Morton and numerous others, all bring back wonderful memories. Dorothy is now deceased as God called her home. She and Hans were wonderful volunteers.

We were doing our best to be the hands and feet of Jesus. Not everyone was or is a "Christian." Many were there for purely humanitarian reasons. Regardless, it was not about us, though it felt like it at times. That must be human nature. Realizing that one could quite literally change the life of an entire family by one simple act of kindness was life changing.

Looking back, I wouldn't have changed anything. One always seeks more. I am sure more would have made me want even more. We helped who we helped. We served who we were able to serve with God's help. We learned, grew and helped others to grow. We made mistakes and had success. We brought the light of Jesus to as many as we could. There are thousands of families across the globe who are better off now than they were before the Mobility Project. In the end, it was good.

Gary Lewallen
Volunteer, retired nurse
Washington

Costa Rica, my first experience. Being the new guy, one has to pay his dues. I'm sure it was with great glee that Steve and Jeff bunked me with Ray Terrill — the legendary snorer of the Mobility Project. The first day, we had a young mother bring her 13-year-old son to a distribution, carrying him in a plastic chair. That is how she packed him around. How thrilled she was to get a wheelchair for him. That was my first experience with the Mobility Project smile.

I remember needing a special-needs chair and going into the container and have God provide just the right one. This happened more than once. I remember looking at the crowd of people waiting and seeing the broken bodies and the families with them. Nobody asked for that, it was a blessing to help them.

Our trip to Thailand was the first time I experienced the sport camps. What fun it was to see the people in wheelchairs learning and having a great time. When you go on a distribution, there is always that element of the unknown. What is the food going to be like, the accommodations, will I have to bunk with Ray again?

We went up to Chiang Mai for the next Thailand distribution. We pulled in off the main street to a hotel that looked fairly nice. We were all on the second or third floors. All was well until the tired missionaries retired at 9:00 P.M. only to be awakened by the disco-tech below with the wafting smells of cigarette smoke coming up the elevator shaft. Of course, we had to check it out. It only lasted until 5:00 A.M.!

We saw so much poverty as we traveled to people's homes to deliver their chairs. They had no way to get to the distribution site. The people were so grateful. This took a lot of time as we had to gather volunteers from the Rotary Club to drive us around. There were no directions, no street signs, no maps, just word of mouth village by village. This was an incredible experience.

Judy Lewallen
Retired, volunteer
Washington

My first trip was to San Bartolo, Mexico, with our church's youth group. The mission we stayed at was absolutely beautiful. That said, you could not flush your toilet paper and had to put it in the garbage pail. Their sewage system is different than ours. I was glad to have my son Aaron on this trip as well as our good friends Billie and Miquela.

We got to walk through the cornfields to where the Masowa Indians had a pottery and stained-glass studio. I bought several beautiful items at great prices. How I wished for an extra suitcase or two to bring back more. I treasure those pieces still today. Upon taking off from Mexico City on our journey home, we were notified after takeoff that there was debris on the runway. We needed to know what to do to prepare for a crash landing.

Aaron and either pastors Pete or Russ (maybe both of them) were asked to man the chutes if we crash landed. This was so we could quickly and safely get people off the plane. Talk about being confronted with one's mortality. There were some scared kids. We made it home safe after all was said and done. What a joy to be used by God to bless another with mobility!

I recall staying at a Pastor's retreat center in Costa Rica. It was a very pretty accommodation. The Mobility Project had a good set up with people like Adilita. She worked with Focus on the Family, a nonprofit Christian organization. They would fill out the applications in-country and have the people in need ready to go.

We worked with the Costa Rica Rotary Club. They helped us to seat all the people in the wheelchairs. I can still see Adilita driving the

Mercedes van around curvy roads by the terraced hillside coffee fields with one hand on the wheel and the other on her phone. I was blown away by the locals' use of their horns. They blew their horn not to give someone heck but to get their attention so they could move ahead and merge in or check if it was ok to pass them.

Our accommodations in Mazatlan, Mexico, were not near as nice as the previous trips. We stayed in a large open rehab gym. Some of us were off in one large separate room that was refitted (duct-taped) with long sheets of plastic in an attempt to hold in the cool air of the makeshift air conditioner. It was so hot.

Jeff and Lisa had to sleep in the gym where they hung curtains up for privacy. They just had a fan. The temperature was over 100 degrees every day. This place was also a working rehab center with clients visiting on a daily basis. They took care of children with disabilities and we also sat children in wheelchairs.

We also did a vacation bible school for the children. We all went to a worship service together. There were quite a few people. When we all sang together, most in Spanish and us in English, you could feel the Holy Spirit in our midst. It was a goosebump-down-the-spine experience. It drove home to me that we are all just one very big human family!

Bridgette Turner
World Access Project volunteer

"My group gave a wheelchair to an 84-year-old woman who suffers with Alzheimer's. She is a shell of a woman who hasn't walked in many, many years due to her poor health. She isn't able to even form a word.

After filling out the paperwork, it was time for her chair. Prior to getting her seated in a wheelchair, her daughter carried her everywhere. At the distribution, her daughter gently scooped her mother up in her arms and delicately placed her in her wheelchair. I immediately began to sob. This tearing experience continued for over 30 minutes while I held her hand and waited for the team picture and prayer in front of the banner of the World Access Project.

I knelt at her feet and wheels, holding her hand and watched her peacefully close her eyes and nod her head. Unexpectedly, she leaned forward and her opposite hand reached out to touch my curly hair.

After the picture and paperwork, I waited with her outside for their taxi. Another volunteer translated for me and her daughter. Another

20 minutes of joyful, loving tears. That was the highlight of my day. Third World issues are real. Problems at home seem so much smaller."

Looking back I recall many experiences. Reading what our friends wrote brought joy to my heart and caused me to reflect back and remember many specific stories. I remembered Afghanistan. Little Agomah, 7 years old, and her father who carried her several miles in hopes she might receive a wheelchair. She simply had a high fever at 6 months old and they could not obtain medical treatment.

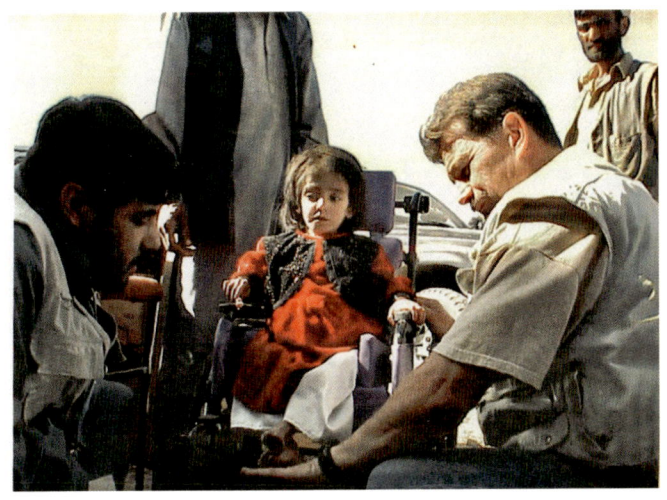

Jeff and Mahboob seating Agomah

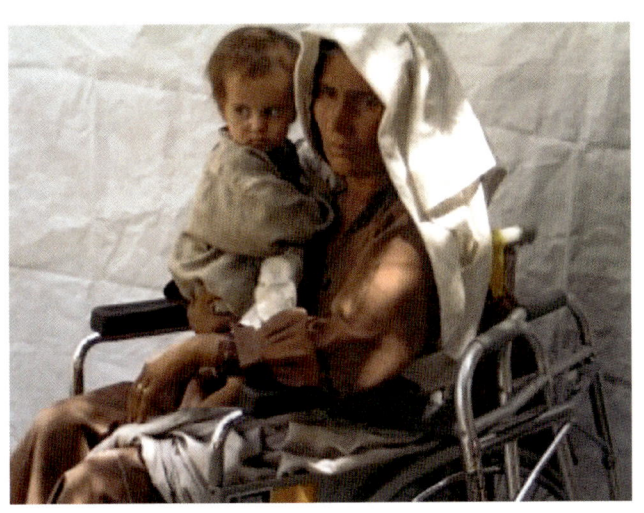

Homeless woman in Afghanistan wanting to give us her child.

Working in the poorest countries on the planet can give one a real sense of appreciation for the conveniences we take for granted every day here at home.

Vietnam. Martin from Colorado Springs hugging a man who he had just helped seat in a wheelchair. They served in the Vietnam war on opposite sides. Martin said this was the most healing experience he had had since he came back from the war. After many tears, they prayed together.

We were blessed to be able to do this work when we were still in our 40s. Most people wait until they retire to start volunteering and traveling the world. God knew that was not in our plan. There were people who came with us that were believers. Some who were not but they left the outreach with a new sense or awakening when it came to God and a new appreciation of life. As a matter of fact, I believe Danny Quintana was not a believer himself. Only he knows what he believes. People saw in us a chance to share Jesus with our acts and not with our words. The servitude displayed, translated everywhere in the world.

Ironically, I am now in a wheelchair part-time due to chronic back pain and several failed surgeries. God enabled us to do unimaginable things at a busy time in our lives when we were at our healthiest. I feel we have had a life that others might dream about as far as experiences.

Yes, we have had the greatest gift of all, the chance to serve God and receive all the blessing. When we lay our heads down at night these are the many faces we see. And oh boy do we have sweet dreams!

Our work resulted in several organizations picking up the Cross and carrying it where we left off. Other people have gotten to enjoy God's love in doing humanitarian work. The World Access Project and PUSH continue our work in Mexico and other countries.

CONCLUSION

"To God belong wisdom and power; counsel and understanding are His."

Job 12:16 NIV

Traveling all over this small planet delivering wheelchairs to the poorest of the poor has been the greatest adventure I ever had. Everyone we have talked with that participated in these wheelchair distributions is grateful for the experience of serving. We have seen the golden temples of Thailand, rode on elephants through the jungles, visited the slave quarters, looked at waterfalls and enjoyed the beautiful sunsets in Sao Tome.

We caught fish off the coast of Mazatlán, Mexico, and fed the volunteers and athletes. We have seen howler monkeys, toucans, iguanas, blue and gold Macaws, humpback whales jumping in the distance, and pelicans diving into the crystal silver blue waters of this beautiful planet. We have watched the dolphins swimming next to us, always curious as to what we are doing on top of their world.

We've witnessed the beauty of God's creation and seen the immense suffering caused primarily by greed, and the lust for money. We visited the genocide museum in Rwanda. We saw the desperation of an amputee crawling on the ground on a piece of cardboard in Afghanistan and a country completely destroyed by war.

When we returned to the United States from distributions all over the world, we witness the petty squabbles of little people. "I'm paying too much for my cable package", "The screen on my phone busted." "I should have bought a much more expensive car." "I don't have enough money for that expensive purse." They just did not get it.

Thanks to the work of brave people like Richard St Denis, public perception has changed. People no longer gawk at us because we are in wheelchairs. People with disabilities are now a common sight. A wheelchair-bound Franklin D. Roosevelt would not be elected president today. But he would not be vilified, either. He would not have to hide his disability like he did while working to overcome the Great Depression and fighting a world war and against the forces of evil and hate. Our society has evolved.

In time, all of us become disabled by the reality called age. How we adjust to disability will depend on our attitude and what opportunities we create for ourselves. Despite less opportunity, we can improve our lives. We are not "victims" or charity cases. No one is going to give it to us. If people with disabilities in poor countries want rights, they will need to fight for them like we did here in the United States.

The only rights you have as human beings are those you are willing to fight for. If you don't have courage, you have already lost your life. Change requires the courage to make a difference. The disabled poor in other countries are just that, brave and smart. They have learned to survive.

Humanitarian work is one big adventure in serving the Lord. We are given the opportunity to serve. We can choose to make a difference or just sit, watch and complain.

We had the good fortune to help deliver wheelchairs to the poorest people all over the world. Now it is time for all poor countries to build wheelchair-manufacturing plants and take care of their own. If you can build a bicycle, you can build a wheelchair. This is not rocket science. We can do this.

Hopefully, one day we will follow the advice of the Lord and truly understand that "the lust for money is truly the root of all evil." Until we learn to control our lust for money, humans will continue to suffer. From landmines sold by people knowing they are harming others, to bombs that take out spinal cords and kill innocent villagers, greed is the evil.

We can follow God's commands of love, charity and forgiveness. We can love life on this planet. The Mobility Project lives in our hearts. The need continues as wars still rage, accidents happen and disease exist. What can be done to help the hundreds of millions of disabled?

We believe families and governments have to take responsibility for their poor, disabled, elderly and those who need mobility. Our military delivers wheelchairs and medical supplies all over the world. But the need is so great. The heavy lifting has to come from the millions of families of the disabled. A little bit of love solves lots of global problems.

We helped thousands of people have better lives. We gave them some mobility and hope. Their faces are etched in our memories forever.

The gratitude of the people whose cross we carried for a few short steps was our thanks and our blessing.

Life is mysterious and at times wonderful. Enjoy these moments. They don't last forever. May all of your moments be filled with joy and the Creator's love. On behalf of all of the volunteers who helped us deliver wheelchairs to the world's poor and disabled, thank you, Lord, for our humanitarian adventures and opportunity to serve.

"To Him belong strength and victory..."

Job 12:13 NIV

The End

About The Authors

Lisa and Jeff Murphy met and grew up in Southern California. Lisa was only 15 and Jeff 18. After a few months they knew they would marry but had to wait until Lisa graduated and was 18 yrs. of age. They were married a week after her graduation. They moved to Arizona shortly after and had 3 children. They now have 7 grandchildren. In 2003 Lisa became the CEO of the Mobility Project, as Jeff continued on the board of directors. This took them all over the world delivering wheelchairs to people in need. Jeff remains a consultant for durable medical equipment companies in Las Vegas Nevada. They look forward to traveling and welcome requests to speak at events. They enjoy spending time on their acreage in Arizona with family and friends riding 4 wheelers and canoeing on the nearby lake. Lisa wants to pursue her passion for photography while working on a 2nd book from their travels. They are passionate about the Lord and look forward to what He has in store for them!

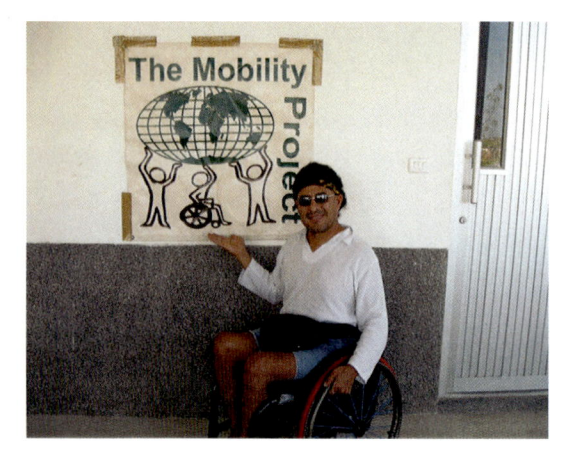

Danny Quintana- is the president and founder of the Global High Seas Marine Preserve, a non-profit education organization dedicated to educating people on ocean wildlife issues. He is the author of several books, most recently *Space and Ocean Exploration: The Alternative to the Military Industrial Complex* and *Copernicus Was Mistaken, Why the Earth is Still the Center of the Universe*. He is a graduate of the University of Utah in political science, B.A. (1980) and Utah's College of Law, J.D. (1983). He is a member of the Mars Society. In college he was a Rockefeller Minority and Hinckley Institute Intern. Mr. Quintana is committed to spending the next 20 years or however long he lives to creating a Global High Seas Marine Preserve. The goal is protect all of the oceans' wildlife. Prior to his creation of this ocean education non-profit, he traveled all over the world with The Mobility Project, a non-profit humanitarian organization. Mr. Quintana continues to practice law, play wheelchair tennis, and write books.